SAVING THE FUTURE

DONNA SINCLAIR

SAVING THE FUTURE

LESSONS IN RESISTANCE FROM YOUNG ACTIVISTS

For Amelia –
with best wishes
for the very best future!

Donna Sinclair

WOOD LAKE

Editor: Mike Schwartzentruber
Proofreader: Dianne Greenslade
Designer: Robert MacDonald

LIBRARY AND ARCHIVES CANADA CATALOGUING IN PUBLICATION
Title: Saving the future : lessons in resistance from young activists /
Donna Sinclair.
Names: Sinclair, Donna, 1943- author.
Description: Includes bibliographical references.
Identifiers: Canadiana (print) 20220234728 | Canadiana (ebook) 20220234795 |
ISBN 9781773432939 (softcover) | ISBN 9781773433974 (HTML)
Subjects: LCSH: Youth – Political activity – Juvenile literature. | LCSH: Political
activists – Biography – Juvenile literature. | LCSH: Political participation – Juvenile
literature. | LCSH: Social action – Juvenile literature. | LCSH: Youth protest
movements – Juvenile literature. | LCGFT: Biographies.
Classification: LCC HQ799.2.P6 S56 2022 | DDC j361.20835 – dc23

The excerpt from "Open Letter from the Williams Family Regarding Their Rights
and Safety," posted October 28, 2020 by the Yellowhead Institute, is reproduced
with the kind permission of the author, Lola Williams.
The photograph of Greta Thunberg is copyright CC-BY-4.0: © European Union
2020 – Source: EP.
The photograph of Robin Wall Kimmerer is by Dale Kakkak.

ISBN 978-1-77343-293-9

Published by Wood Lake Publishing Inc.
485 Beaver Lake Road, Kelowna, BC, Canada V4V 1S5
www.woodlake.com | 250.766.2778

Wood Lake Publishing acknowledges the financial support of
the Government of Canada.
Wood Lake Publishing acknowledges the financial support of the Province of
British Columbia through the Book Publishing Tax Credit.

Wood Lake Publishing acknowledges that we operate in the unceded territory of
the Syilx/Okanagan People, and we work to support reconciliation and challenge
the legacies of colonialism. The Syilx/Okanagan territory is a diverse and beautiful
landscape of deserts and lakes, alpine forests and endangered grasslands.
We honour the ancestral stewardship of the Syilx/Okanagan People.

Printed in Canada
Printing 10 9 8 7 6 5 4 3 2 1

CONTENTS

DEDICATION

To grandchildren, Elijah, Liam, and Jamesie,
and to dear friends' grandchildren,
Philippe and Émilie, Grace and Faye,
Max and Katie, Scott and Beth.
Because you are the future.

Adisclaimer. I'm writing to you both as a grandmother and as someone who tries to be an environmental activist. But I want to be clear that one does not depend on the other. I love my grandkids and I want them to have a healthy world. But even if I had no grandchildren I would still belong to the resistance that the children and youth in this book are leading. Because our earth is so elegant and mysterious in its evolution, and so deeply worthy *in itself* of our passionate love.

That said, I want tell you about our grandson Liam, who lives on the edge of a rainforest in British Columbia. He was watching a nature program when he suddenly jumped up. "Dad, Dad!" he said, "Come quick. The coral reefs are bleaching!"

He was four years old at the time. He had never seen a coral reef. But he knew an emergency when he saw it. And that raises a question for a grandparent (or a parent or a teacher) that we have not really had to face before. What do we tell kids about our climate meltdown? Do we say, "Oh, don't worry. Maybe we can take you to see a reef before they are all gone?" Or "Don't be afraid. That's on the other side of the world. Our waters are perfectly okay." But they're not, of course. And those answers are wrong on so many levels.

In fact, there is no answer to this dilemma, not really. But I think we might worry less about what we tell children and youth, and more about what we do together, *with* them. For instance, when they are little, we might begin by helping them love our Mother Earth. We can picnic and swim and hike in the forest with them – deliberately, consciously, as often as we can.

And as they grow, we might do art with them, because making art empowers everyone, adults and kids. During a four-year battle to prevent TransCanada pipelines from endangering the drinking water of my city, North Bay, a downtown mural was one way our group, Stop Energy East North Bay, called on the power of the arts to help us. There was also the winter day we dramatically skied the spill, kids and adults pouring out on Lake Nipissing, dressed in black to illustrate with our bodies the path of the bitumen from a potential pipeline rupture. There were the movie nights when we watched films about resistance and had discussions afterward. There was the time kids and adults dressed up as drops of water and confronted the pipeline proponents. And there was a cabaret, with song and music and dance and poetry.

Most of all we need to follow our children's lead when their idealism and outrage trumps adult cynicism and doubt. When Greta Thunberg calls us out onto the streets, we need to go with joy. That's especially true during an election period, when a child's honest question – "What are we going to do about the coral reefs?" – requires an equally honest answer from politicians who wish to speak for us in government.

I am very grateful that you are reading the stories in this book. Whether or not you have children, or grandchildren of your own, or hope to have them in the future, or whether you are simply someone else's beloved grandchild (as we all are), it is good to open your heart and to follow the lead of a child. This honours our connection with the earth and with each other.

You've probably heard your grandparents or some "older" person say something like this: "I remember when you could drink water out of the lake." Or "I remember when wildfires weren't so bad."

My grandchildren and their friends often hear this kind of talk. They're polite about it, reminding me only once in a while that they have heard this before, maybe yesterday. And they have things they talk about, too. Faye, at ten, listing things she was thankful for, included "the chance to see the world before it ends. Seeing all the animals before they are extinct."

When I hear children and teens express things like that, I become deeply troubled, so I decided to write this book. Because I actually *do* remember a time, a world in which you could drink out of the lake, and people knew what the songs of certain birds sounded like, and the only thing we thought about coral reefs was that we dreamed of snorkelling in them one day.

Also, I wrote this book because I am an activist. In order to save the future, I believe we have to actively try to prevent dangers such as global warming and water contamination and habitat loss for wild animals.

I have stood in the cold many times – all day – with a candle, trying to keep it from blowing out in the bitter, frigid, terrible wind, trying to persuade my member of Parliament that we should ban land mines or nuclear weapons. Where I live, it's generally well below freezing in winter. (Oh, except now, because of climate change.) Also, I have semi-ruined many otherwise fun parties by talking loudly about tar sands pipelines. (I try not to do this.) I have been arrested while peacefully protesting on Parliament Hill.

Sometimes I did these things because young people did them first. I saw teenagers on the news being arrested in front of the White House for protesting a pipeline. My young daughter was dumped out of her boat into the ocean and arrested (dripping wet) for filming the harassment of Indigenous lobster fishers by the RCMP. How could I not copy their determination and courage?

And I was *copying* their courage because I am not brave. I am shy and introverted. I would much rather read a book about a kick-ass heroine than be one.

But I love trees and rocks, lakes and rivers, oceans and beaches, grasslands and mountains. I love cities with big green parks and leafy neighbourhoods and great schools. And I want the forests, the water, the plains, and the cities to be healthy and strong and safe and beautiful for all who live in them.

Many children and teens are already standing up for all these things. That's because children have powers – such as the overwhelming need to speak up when something is very wrong – that adults sometimes lose. I have talked to some of them and offer their stories and advice here. I have added some of my own. I hope that these ten lessons, offered humbly from a 20th-century kid, who grew into a 21st-century "Nana," will help save the future.

ONE

NAHIRA GERSTER-SIM

SEE CLEARLY, GET THE VOTE

When Nahira Gerster-Sim was seven years old, she went to the MacMillan Space Centre in Vancouver with her family. It was everything a seven-year-old hopes for – rockets and maps and pictures of outer space. But when she found her way into a video presentation on the universe, it all became background noise. Nahira discovered that Earth is going to blow up. Not for a few billion years, of course. But for her, the time Earth had left didn't matter. What *did* matter was that it was going to happen.

Years later when Nahira was 16, she looked back at that moment when she was seven and realized that was when she saw clearly that "the earth will not last forever." It was a "defining moment" in her life.

For Nahira, "seeing clearly" did not mean being paralyzed by fear. Instead, she began to make choices to "help Earth, given its limited time." She got involved in fighting climate change. She became a vegan. Soon she saw that youth everywhere, as a group, were more interested in climate action than many adults – maybe because they are the ones who will have to live with the consequences of doing nothing.

Nine years after she "totally freaked out" in the space centre, Nahira helped found Vote16BC because she saw very clearly that to change the world you must make its political leaders listen to you.

Adults – including the ones in government with MLA or MP after their names – can get used to believing that climate change is unstoppable. Others think it does not exist, or that we can figure out how to live with it. Some adults don't seem to mind that many animals go extinct each year and that the problem will only get worse if we don't do something. Or they can't imagine a way to live without burning gas and oil and coal, even though that hurts Earth's atmosphere. Above all, they can't imagine young people saying what they think by voting.

Nahira and her friends get frustrated when they are not consulted about matters that directly affect them. This includes what they are taught in school. "I don't get to have any say about the curriculum. It is decided without consultation and without my permission," said Nahira. "There's not a lot in it about climate change or democracy."

For Nahira and the other founders of Vote16BC, the solution is the ballot box, the chance to vote in government elections. The votes of youth who are 16 years old or older can influence the way governments behave. They can push politicians in a different direction. For instance, Nahira says that "we need to create policy that is not just targeted at making the most money or having corporations on our side." Youth will be around much longer than most people who are now creating all the rules and regulations. So "let the future decide the future."

Even without the vote, children and teens know the world's problems. They are already telling governments what to focus on. "Youth climate strikes, Fridays for the Future – this is our way of telling government their climate policy is not okay."

But not everyone agrees youth should be able to vote. One argument against giving 16-year-olds this democratic right is that "young people don't vote" anyway. Nahira doesn't buy that argument. "There are plenty of countries, like Scotland, where 16-year-olds are voting," she says. Also, she believes children are more stable in terms of their life journey than they will be in a few years. While "people who are 18 to 25 years old are in a transition phase, figuring out what this whole adult life is like," most 16-year-olds are still at home with their families. "That would be a good point to enter politics," she says, "because once you develop the habit of voting, you continue."

Another argument against Vote16BC members hear is that "we will just vote the way our parents tell us to." Not necessarily. Nahira points to school climate strikes and gun control marches, where children have made up their own minds about what they believe and where they stand. "Our values are strong and clear," she says. Further, "we will vote to improve our education," giving children even more ability to think clearly, for themselves.

Nahira and her friends present their own arguments in favour of Vote16BC. In many places, you can marry, join the army, and drive a car at 16. Why not vote? In fact, the same arguments against allowing 16-year-olds to vote were once made by men against women. Many years ago, people who didn't want women to vote said that women would only vote the way their husbands told them to. Some people even said that women didn't know enough or weren't experienced enough to vote.

YOUTH ARE EDUCATING THEMSELVES

The COVID-19 quarantines and lockdowns of 2020 and 2021 have meant time and space to "open our eyes" even more fully, says Nahira. Now their group is determined to stand in solidarity with Black and Indigenous youth, and to "raise a storm of activism and justice seeking." And youth are educating them-

PERSISTENCE PAYS OFF

In November 2019, Mira Blakely, Nahira's colleague in Vote16BC, went to the NDP (New Democratic Party) political convention in British Columbia to argue that 16-year-olds should have the vote. She and her friends worked hard all weekend, talking to as many delegates as they could about why this is important. Soon, adult delegates were going to the microphones to argue in their favour. They held up signs. Mira talked to the premier of British Columbia and asked for his help. Eventually, the delegates to the NDP convention voted unanimously that the voting age in the province should be 16.

But Mira still did not just relax.

She found the premier again and pointed out that they had the delegates' support. She wanted a clear answer, she told him. Mira was 15 and she was bravely talking to the political leader of the province. "Will you look into this?" she asked. He said that he would.

Later, the group made an excellent video promoting Vote16BC. Everybody who spoke on the video added more information about their concerns. Mira explained why they are working so persistently now. It's time for change, she said, "to really get our voices heard. It is more important than ever to see youth voices amplified and our issues addressed."

selves to do so. Nahira describes the way fast fashion hurts Earth, the way even the colour of blue jeans hurts the water in Thailand and Africa. We are "treating our planet so badly," she says. "We push our manufacturing out onto other people and call ourselves green and developed."

First though, the Vote16BC team is determined to get to a place where they can influence decision-makers. They are training people across the province to help campaign for the vote, and already have endorsements from the city of Vancouver, the British Columbia Teachers' Federation, and the Union of BC Municipalities.

None of this is easy. Activism means keeping our eyes open and seeing things that might upset us – just like Nahira at the space centre when she was seven years old. It means working hard to change the minds of adults about climate change or species loss while knowing that kids shouldn't have to do

THE NAKED EMPEROR

The power of children and youth to name the truth, even one that is painful or embarrassing, is one that adults often lose growing up. Like the child in the folk tale about the emperor who had been fooled into believing he was wearing exquisite clothes when he was really naked. All the grownups went along with the king, pretending he had clothes on commenting on how beautiful they were. Perhaps they worried that the king would punish them or even execute them if they told the truth. But a small child, giggling wildly, pointed out the obvious. Unfortunately, the story ends there. But surely, since the entire kingdom had burst into delighted laughter, the king slunk away in humiliation, and nobody was hurt. Truth-telling is one antidote to bullying.

this. It's not fair to have to clean up a mess you didn't make.

The upside is the hope and confidence that shines so brightly in Nahira. She is respectful even to politicians who are less knowledgeable than she and her friends are. Above all, she is clear-eyed. She sees the world the way it is and does not get used to it. That is one of the gifts that children and youth bring to activism.

WHAT WE CAN LEARN FROM NAHIRA

Nahira says, "You feel a lot of things going wrong with the world, and you see all the racism. It's a lot. It's not something you shouldn't know. You should know it, but it takes away from that idealistic childhood, the fun and games. It sucks that we have to be so involved because we have to fix this, so our children don't have to be worried about clean water and police brutality every single day.

Figure out what you are passionate about. It is hard to be an activist if you don't know what your core values are. Second, find people who are going to support you. Activism is not possible alone. It's all about co-operation with other people, even if it is finding that connection through social media. And third, don't give up. There are so many hurdles and it is going to take a lot of work. I spend a lot of time writing emails. It is easy to say I have other more important things in life. But what you tell yourself is, it is important to keep going."

TWO

SOPHIA MATHUR

KNOW YOUR RIGHTS AND FIGHT FOR THEM

Sophia Mathur was drawing pictures while her mom was in a meeting. Her mom was working hard, trying to tell politicians to do more to heal the climate. Sophia was only seven, but she was very good at drawing cats. One of her drawings was called *A Carbon Tax Is a Purr-fect solution*. Later, she talked with her mom: "Can I go with you to Ottawa?" she asked. Not too long after, Sophia and her mom travelled to the capital from their home in Sudbury, Ontario. Sophia was having an exciting time on Parliament Hill. They were standing with a huge crowd demanding climate action from the government. She thought these politicians might have children of their own and so it was important for her to be there. Sophia was doing her best to help the planet.

Four years later, when Sophia was 11, she heard about Greta Thunberg's school strikes for the climate. Every Friday, Greta had been sitting in front of the Swedish Parliament buildings instead of going to school. Sophia too took Fridays off school with her friends. They were part of Fridays for Future, which is growing all over the world. They made signs and got others to come together in a park in downtown Sudbury. Not long after that, she and six others, backed by the environmental law organization EcoJustice, decided to sue the new provincial government in Ontario. When the Progressive Conservative party came into office it tore down windmills. It wanted to build more highways, even through

---

KIDS TAKING GOVERNMENTS TO COURT

All over the world, children are now turning to the courts to claim their right to a healthy future. Sometimes they win. Sometimes they lose. Even when they lose, people are listening to them. Here are just a few examples.

In **Portugal,** in 2020, six children and young adults – aged eight to 21 – sued 33 countries in Europe because they have not done enough to fight climate change. Their argument (that this is against their human rights) is going to the European Court of Human Rights in Strasbourg, France. "It terrifies me," says one of them, "that the record-breaking heat waves we have endured are only the beginning. We have so little time to stop this."

In **Colombia**, in 2019, 25 youth sued their government for not protecting the part of the Amazon rainforest that is in their country. They won. The court agreed that both their rights and that of the rainforest were being hurt by too many trees being cut down.

In **The Netherlands**, a winning lawsuit by children in 2019 (it finally involved 900 citizens) led to a court order for the government to deeply cut carbon emissions.

In the **United States**, 21 children sued their government in 2015. They said they were being deprived of their "right to life" because they were losing a climate system capable of sustaining human life. (In the United States, citizens cannot be deprived of life, liberty, or property without "due process of law.") When the case finally got to court, they lost. But they are taking another step, called "appealing," which means they will go to a higher, more powerful court to try again.

the precious Greenbelt, a protected area of green space, farmland, forests, wetlands, and watersheds the runs for hundreds of kilometres in Southern Ontario. In spite of the increased flooding climate change will bring, it has weakened laws that protect the wetlands that help prevent floods.

In the minds of these politicians, a warming planet does not seem to be a worry, so Sophia and her friends are taking them to court to change their minds. "It's not fair," she said, that the planet where she and her friends are growing up is "not going to be safe. They are not respecting our rights. They are not listening to us."

But *do* kids have rights? *Should* adults listen to children? When they grow up, do adults forget to respect children's ability to see and speak the truth?

CHILDREN HAVE RIGHTS

According to the United Nations, children do have rights – 54 of them, to be exact. In the *United Nations Convention on the Rights of the Child*, Article 3, for instance, says "All adults should do what is best for you." Article 4 says that the government "has a responsibility" to make sure your rights are protected. Article 12 says that you "have the right to give your opinion, and for adults to listen and take it seriously."

Canada has signed on to the agreement that says all this. Yes, good idea, said our leaders. In fact, in 2017 our government supported a student committee (with lots of kids on it) that studied the agreement and even asked for improvements. Unfortunately, governments make promises, but don't always fulfill·them.

Other agreements also say that governments have to stand up for all their citizens, including kids. If our governments don't do what they promised, then judges can order them to keep their promises. Sophia and her friends are asking a judge to order Ontario to honour their rights, promised in the *Canadian Charter of Rights and Freedoms*. These rights are just as important as the ones in the *United Nations Convention on the Rights of the Child*, and children are entitled to them like every other citizen. We all have a right to "life, liberty, and security of the person," for example.

But Sophia and her friends point out that the Ontario government is weakening efforts to save the climate. Can you imagine trying to bike or run in

POLITICIANS CAN BE ALLIES FOR CHILDREN

Sophia and her allies (friends and supporters) in Fridays for Future in Sudbury know how to get politicians to listen. Even during the pandemic, they set up Zoom calls with leaders in their area – the mayor, members of Parliament, senators, and others – to talk about climate change. For example, they talked about how climate change connects to the United Nations' declaration about Indigenous people's rights. When it comes to rights, Sophia's group doesn't leave anyone out. Later, they celebrated the United States rejoining the Paris Accord (that's a big agreement about climate action) when President Biden took office. In summer, again despite the pandemic, they even managed to gather outdoors for rallies, and they persuaded some politicians to dance with them.

"We are grateful," says Sophia, "for the politicians' time, for listening to us and dancing with us. This is what democracy looks like: community members listening to each other."

overwhelming heat? Can you imagine the stress of watching your house burn down in a wildfire? What if you couldn't get clean drinking water because there were algae blooms all over your lake? Or what about ticks? Ticks are tiny eight-legged bugs that bite. If untreated, those bites can make a person sick with something called Lyme Disease. In North America, ticks live in fields and forests, where people like to hike. Because of climate change, the number of ticks

BILLION-DOLLAR COMPANY NEEDS MONEY FROM ... FOUR TEENAGERS?

Four teenagers in British Columbia also started a lawsuit. Calling themselves Youth Stop TMX, they tried to stop a new pipeline from being built beside an old one. One of the four, 13-year-old Rebecca Wolf Gage, says that "this pipeline and the oil that flows through it is destroying my future." It is the same message that Sophia and her friends are spreading in Ontario. In this case, the pipeline would allow more tar sands oil to be burned. This means more greenhouse gas emissions. Which means more (wait for it) climate change. This is not healthy for children, and it's not healthy for adults and animals either.

Unfortunately, the Youth Stop TMX lawsuit did not succeed. The court refused to hear it. Even worse, the court granted the company that is building the pipeline "costs." That means when the company (Trans Mountain Pipeline ULC) demanded that the four teenagers pay all its legal bills for this case, the judge agreed.

The year before, Trans Mountain Pipeline ULC made $137.8 million. That's a lot more than babysitting money! Fortunately, when an online newspaper called *The National Observer* asked the corporation about it, the company suddenly decided it didn't need to have their bills paid by children. That shows that even large companies don't like to look greedy. The ability to point out what is truly ridiculous is one of the unique powers children have. If you grow up to be a zillionaire, you might lose that ability. Try not to.

is growing. Imagine being too worried about Lyme disease to hike in the woods. That is not security of person!

EVERYONE THE SAME BEFORE THE LAW

Another right we all have is "equality before the law" regardless of race, colour, religion, and age. Yes, *age*. It's right there in our Charter. Even when we are very young (or in my case, very old) we are entitled to equal protection. As climate change gets worse, that does not work out very well for children. Even if governments make changes now – for example by banning gas-powered cars after 2030 – many older people will be dead before things get really bad, or before the changes begin to make things better. But people who are children now will still be alive, and they will be the ones who have to deal with more large floods or ice storms or tornadoes. They'll also need to care for people who are fleeing to Canada from other parts of the world that are too hot to live in anymore.

So it is good that Sophia and her friends have won the right to be heard in court. Their lawyers will argue that the government of Ontario needs to fix this. Now!

Going to court is a brave thing for Sophia and her friends to do because – surprise – lawsuits cost money and although Ecojustice is helping them, children don't have as much money as governments do. What children *do* have is the power to draw attention to large governments who neglect the rights of small people instead of doing their job, which is to make sure everyone is safe. Perhaps when voters

see this they will think "We don't want any more of
this!" and elect a new government.

WHAT WE CAN LEARN FROM SOPHIA

Sophia says, "Take your fear and anger and use it as
a weapon. Turn it into hope and action. Bring your
passion into the climate movement. I am passionate
about dance. We have even got politicians to dance
for the climate. Every voice matters. Post a poem or
a piece of art. Sometimes art can speak more than
words do.

We need to listen to Indigenous people. They have
knowledge of the earth. And it's great to make new
friends.

You can't trust just social media. I know people
who study climate change, experts at the university.
I trust those people and the science."

THREE

KAIDEN PELDJAK AND KILE GEORGE

BE AN ANTI-RACISM ALLY

A sunny day, hot for early summer. North Bay, Ontario, just like other parts of the world, was in the midst of the new COVID-19 pandemic. Most people were staying quietly in their homes, worried about a virus that nobody understood very well. But the month before, in May, a Black man named George Floyd had been killed by a white police officer in Minneapolis, in the United States. The officer kneeled on his neck for almost nine minutes, ignoring George's pleas that he could not breathe. Protests began immediately, the largest ever seen in the United States.

Protests soon started around the world. In North Bay, far away from Minneapolis, two high school students named Kaiden Peldjak and Kile George both felt that "something needed to be done," to use Kaiden's words. "*Anything* needed to be done." Both were on the student council, they were good friends, and they were used to organizing stuff. "We knew it would be up to us," said Kile, "or someone like us." Kaiden is Black. Kile is Indigenous.

Right away they got to work and organized a march. Over 2,000 people marched – kids and adults, old and young. In fact, it was the largest protest to ever happen in North Bay. Just as incredible, people walked despite their fears. They wore masks and gloves as protection from the virus and hats as protection from the sun. Families held hands while others tried to stay carefully apart. They all marched to city hall, determined to "honour the lives of those who have passed over countless years of police brutality and racism." Like white and Indigenous and Black and Asian people all over the world who were also walking and protesting together, the people in

---

COLONIALISM

"Colonialism" is as powerful a word as racism. They go together. Colonialism means taking over other peoples' land and doing what you like with it. In Canada, one result of colonialism was that Indigenous children were taken away from their parents. For about 100 years, starting in the mid-1800s and going until the mid-1900s, children as young as five or six were forced to go to residential schools.

Imagine you are an Indigenous child. You are taken from your family and your friends and have to stay for years in a large school where the teachers speak a different language and don't let you speak your own language. If you have a brother or sister in the same school, you aren't allowed to talk to them. The teachers will probably cut off all your hair and shave your head. In the worst schools, there was always danger from disease, hunger, and very harsh punishment. Everything was designed to make you forget your language – to forget who you are – and to train you to grow up to be a farmhand or a household servant. These residential schools were an important part and example of colonialism.

Another way to understand colonialism is that it is when powerful people from a different country or culture want everyone else to live by their rules or to live like they do. You might think colonialism is over. It is not. An example of colonialism today, is when big mining companies dig up Indigenous lands even when Indigenous people don't want them to.

North Bay made speeches and sang songs.

Kaiden and Kile were very surprised by the turn-out. They had not expected even 200 people. "I'm not sure we knew what we were signing up for," Kile says now. But "it was so beautiful to be part of something like that. And then, during a song, we kneeled. And then everyone else kneeled. And that felt like a moment of accomplishment because ... oh ... we actually did something." Kile pauses. "There's this saying, 'Be the change you want to see in the world.' I really want to see things firsthand. I can't just wait for someone else to do it."

As Kaiden says, "It was just part of this world project that was going on, part of a much bigger change, not just in North Bay." Millions of people were all trying to be good allies in a very long and very large effort to stop the bullying we call racism.

HOW TO BECOME AN ALLY

Trying to end racism – the idea that one group of people is somehow better (or worse) than another group – means, first, learning some new words. These words describe things that happen to many Black and Indigenous children, even when they are very young.

LEARN ABOUT MICRO-AGGRESSIONS

Kaiden says there are a lot of different little mo-ments – like "how someone holds themselves differ-ently when you come into the room," or "how the security guard might loop around and follow you when you at the mall" – that are hurtful. It's "not natural," says Kile, "to be constantly trying to protect ourselves and looking for ways to be safe." Those quiet little attacks are different for everyone. Maybe it's when a teacher looks past a Black kid and calls on a white kid, even though both kids have their hands up and know the answer. Over and over. (Important note: Not all teachers are like this.) Or maybe a friend is having a birthday party and you are not invited, even though you enjoy each other's company. Or maybe people comment on your hair. If these things happen to you day after day after day, they affect you. You might begin to wonder why people think you aren't as good as they are.

LEARN ABOUT PRIVILEGE

Many white kids experience the exact opposite of micro-aggressions, especially if they have nice clothes. They get invited to all the birthday parties, and sleepovers, and dances. The teacher pays attention to them. If this happens to you over and over, it is easy to believe you deserve this. You never even notice that you are beginning to believe you are entitled to this special treatment.

LEARN TO SEE BULLYING

Racism is another word for bullying. It means, for example, that Black teenagers (especially boys) who are learning to drive also have to learn about the extra dangers they may face if they are stopped by some police. Racism means that Indigenous teens (especially girls) who must leave their home communities to go to school have to learn the extra dangers they may face from some boys and men who are bullies.

First, if you are not Indigenous or Black, it takes work to understand what those words "micro-aggression" and "privilege" actually mean. You need to be able to put yourself in someone else's shoes, which is not easy. You have to listen very carefully to what your friends say to you about their lives. Being a good ally is personal. And it's a process. It goes on and on. You don't just become one in a day.

Second, a good ally learns to watch their language. Kaiden says to watch for words that push people of different colours further apart: for example, if a white kid describes my friend as my "*Black friend*" – which highlights the difference.

Third, a good ally needs to "watch and ask directly what their friends who are people of colour need," says Kaiden. But then, think before you speak. Even though "white voices have to be brought into the mix" they don't always have to be the "loudest voices in the room." If you are a white kid, listen and be quiet sometimes.

In fact, if you are a little kid who is trying to be a good ally, you may just have to watch and listen and learn for quite a while, says Kaiden. If those micro-aggressions are coming from an adult and you "try to interrupt, something good could happen. On the other hand, it could backfire." It's no fun being sent out of class. And, Kile adds sympathetically and wisely, kids who are really young "have no idea racism is a thing. They haven't really formed the concept in their mind – and we are asking them to avoid it?"

Everyone, young and old, should just name bullying when we see it, because that too is what racism is, and we all know about it at a young age. Maybe we can gather up some friends, and maybe parents, and speak to the adult in charge together, quietly, about how important it is to treat all people, but kids especially, the same.

Both Kile and Kaiden agree on this: the cure for racism is to open your mind to different world views and your heart to empathy (which means allowing yourself to imagine and feel what someone else is feeling).

It is also important to know that people hold a lot of anger from our history together, from "what the larger white collective has done," says Kile. But it's not "as if people of colour are demanding they pay them back, personally." They are not. But they do need friends and allies to listen and to help make their voices stronger and reach farther. As they grow older and more confident, white kids can begin to take on the job that white people need to do – taking apart the things that separate and hurt people, and then rebuilding those things, only much better.

RECONCILIATION

For white children and youth, this may be the hardest lesson of all – learning about reconciliation. That is the work that must be done so white and Indigenous or Black people can care for each other and be respectful and kind to one another. We cannot be good friends and love each other if things are not fair. Terrible things happened before our time. That's not our fault. But reconciliation still has to happen. Terrible things are still happening, like the murder of George Floyd. That's not our fault either. But reconciliation is still our responsibility if we are white. Because if someone is white, they are growing up with advantages other people don't have. Until that stops, we can't heal the world.

When Kile and Kaiden planned their march, their non-Black and non-Indigenous friends helped with organizing and by making posters. Then lots and lots of people, young and old – who didn't even know Kile and Kaiden – got out and marched. By doing that, they made the voices of Kile and Kaiden much louder and much stronger. *That's* being a good ally.

OTHER THINGS TO LEARN

How to be uncomfortable. Sometimes people who have never been listened to have a lot to say, and you're the only one around to hear. It's important to listen respectfully, even if it makes you uncomfortable.

How to look inside, see your own racism, admit it, and try to overcome it. It's hard to see your own flaws, but everyone has them, so you're not alone.

How to give away your own privilege, if you have some. Sometimes simply standing beside someone who often gets overlooked means you get overlooked, too. That's giving away some of your privilege.

How to interrupt. Sometimes people tell jokes or say awful things about other people without even knowing they are being mean. You can say, "Wait!" or "I don't think that's funny," or "When you say things like that, it hurts because it is not true."

How to talk to people (maybe in your own family) you disagree with. You can say what you think, kindly and firmly. If they still disagree, you can say, "Well, let's agree to disagree on this, and still be friends." People do not always agree, but they should hear different ideas.

ALLIES WORKING TOGETHER IN SOLIDARITY
Notes from Idle No More

One time that allies and Indigenous people really worked together was a few years ago, during the demonstrations against broken promises known as Idle No More. Four women – two Indigenous, two non-Indigenous – started the demonstrations, and they spread across Canada. This is my diary of what it was like in my area.

Day One: Sunday

Tonight I went with friends to an Idle No More planning meeting held by the youth at Nipissing First Nation, near North Bay, Ontario. It felt good to go, as a non-Indigenous person, and be welcomed.

One of the youth described his visit with Chief Theresa Spence. She has been fasting for weeks, trying to persuade the Governor General and the prime minister to meet with First Nations leaders about the treaties our government has dishonoured.

The visit was only for a few minutes, he said, but he was clearly moved. "I would put her up there with my grandmother, and my mother."

Many elders were at this meeting too. They spoke in support, from their hearts.

Liaison officers from the Ontario Provincial Police and officers from both North Bay and the Anishinabek police outlined their plans to keep everyone safe during the demonstrations. It gives me hope that all our relationships can become healthy and whole.

Day Three: Tuesday

Today I participated in a peaceful slow-down of traffic on
Highway 17 (the King's Highway, as one elder referred to it on
Sunday). It was -3 C and I had double-layered and worn my
warmest parka, but the day was grey and I was cold. I found
myself smiling like a crazy person, though. I don't know why.
Maybe it was the joy surrounding me, so many people (including several who, like us, are not Indigenous) so full of determination.

Or maybe it was the pleasure of holding up a sign complaining about damage to water. Or maybe it was the motor-
ists, most accepting the information pamphlets the youth
handed them, honking and waving cheerfully as they drove
away.

Maybe I was smiling because of the warm bannock
someone brought around. Or maybe it was because I had a
chance to stand in solidarity, a chance to say that broken
promises do not take place in my name.

Day Four: Wednesday

Glorious sunny day. A large group from the Nipissing and Dokis
First Nations, with many non-Indigenous supporters, held a
round dance at the corner of Highway 17 and Highway 11. First,
we marched up Algonquin Avenue, carrying flags and banners,
chatting, cheering. When the marchers chanted, "We are
Indian, we are proud," I was politely silent. When we got there,
I held hands in the circle and shuffled awkwardly along to the
drumbeat. White person dancing! And smiling. So many
children, so many elders, so much joy.

A PRIVILEGE QUIZ

Have you ever had

- a stranger tell you to "go back where you came from"?
- a security guard watch you closely at the store, or even follow you around?
- someone call you a rude nickname?
- someone be surprised when you did well on a test?
- your name constantly confused with the only other person of your colour in the group?
- someone ask you where you are *actually* from?
- someone say that your name is hard to pronounce?
- someone ask, "Why do you wear that"?
- someone tell you your food is strange, or smells bad?
- an adult – even one unknown to you – touch your hair?

These things happen to many people. If they have *never* happened to you, you might consider that you have privilege. Even if you didn't ask for it. You don't have to feel guilty. You just need to make sure you think more and be more caring or empathetic than the people who made these things happen.

FOUR

GRETA THUNBERG

SHOW UP

It was three weeks before a national election in Sweden, and Greta Thunberg felt she had to do something. She was frightened and getting angrier all the time. Ever since she was nine, in Grade 3, she had known about climate change. But nobody, not even the people in the government, ever really talked a lot about it. Even though the damage it will cause, and was already causing, is so huge. Greta has discovered that the earth, especially its atmosphere, is in trouble. Humans have caused the problem. But they really aren't doing enough to solve it.

Greta was 15 when she got on her bike and rode to the Swedish Parliament. It sits on an island in a lake in the middle of the city of Stockholm. It was a school day. Although they respect her research, her parents thought she should be in school. But Greta decided she had to do something. She locked her bike to a railing, walked over the bridge to the island, and sat down on the steps of the Parliament building which is made from beautiful reddish-grey granite. Then she propped her homemade sign beside her: "School Strike for the Climate." She also had with her 100 leaflets with facts about global warming to hand out. She was alone.

The next day she got up and did the same thing. She rode her bike to Parliament. This time she remembered to bring a cushion because the steps were hard. A few people decided to join her, first children, then some adults. Each day more people arrived and joined her. They all talked to each other and posted about their strike on Twitter and Instagram. Soon some members of Parliament were saying hello as they passed by, and more reporters came to write stories about this girl who was skipping school for the climate.

A few years before she did all this, Greta had been very depressed. When she was 11, she had stopped talking and started to cry much of the time. She went over a year without talking. She didn't eat much. Her worried parents discovered that she was on the autism spectrum. In her case, that means she finds it impossible to turn away and think about other things when she is focused on something she knows is important.

Greta eventually changed schools and started to talk with others about the climate. That's when she heard about students in the United States who were speaking out about gun laws in that country. It's also when she stopped crying.

Today Greta knows what she has to say and says it so clearly and bravely, with so much knowledge and conviction, that adults and leaders around the world have begun to listen. So have other children and youth.

All around the world the children and youth by

the thousands and then the millions have begun to skip school on certain Fridays, striking for the climate, because Greta is not the only one who is frightened, angry, and knowledgeable. Many other people – maybe including you – are frightened, angry, and knowledgeable, too. They are all speaking out.

Greta, joined by other young leaders, has now spoken to the United Nations, to the World Economic Forum, to great crowds in capital cities, and to the media. And people are listening.

WHAT WE CAN LEARN FROM GRETA
It isn't easy being Greta. She is shy and soft-spoken, except when she is firmly telling the truth to leaders who would rather not hear it. She is not keen to be the centre of attention, but we can learn so much from her.

Actions are better than words alone
Even though Greta is very good at speaking, she really began to make a difference when she took her schoolbooks, her sign, and her lunch, and cycled to the place where the nation's leaders were meeting. She studied her books, but she had made herself *visible*. Day after day, she showed up. Showing up may be the most important action of all.

Obedience has to make sense
World leaders weren't too pleased when hundreds of thousands and then millions of children followed Greta's example of skipping school to strike for the climate. In fact, many were downright angry or grumpy about it. Theresa May, Britain's prime min-

ister, said that the climate marchers' "disruption increases teachers' workloads and wastes lesson time." Australia's prime minister, Scott Morrison, said kids have "enough things to be anxious about. We've got to let kids be kids." When Donald Trump was president of the United States – possibly the most powerful man in the world – he called Greta "ridiculous" on Twitter and told her to "work on her Anger Management problem, then go to a good old-fashioned movie with a friend!" These leaders and so many others like them command the obedience of billions of people, including armies. Greta simply refused to obey any of them. She just obeys the science that is telling her the world is in trouble.

We have to name evil
Greta once told the world's most powerful people who were meeting in Davos, Switzerland, that she wanted them to panic, to take action, to "behave as if you are in the middle of a crisis." (Perhaps if you are very rich it is more difficult to see a crisis, because it may not touch you immediately.) In another world meeting, where leaders discussed climate change but then dined on steak and watched jets in aerial displays, she posted angrily on social media, pointing out their lack of responsibility when "our house, planet earth is going up in flames." Giving money to fossil fuel companies, pushing pipelines through land that is not yours, and letting the Amazon rainforest burn are wicked acts because they contribute to the destruction of Earth. We have to name that fact.

The most terrible situation can turn around

Greta's family was in turmoil with her depression and her younger sister's rages and terrible sensitivity to sound. Then her parents discovered that both Greta and her sister, Beata, are on the autism spectrum. They were exhausted with worry about them, even as they diligently studied to learn what Greta already knew about the climate. Everybody was trying very hard, but the family lived with anguish and chaos much of the time. (The family describes this in their book *Our House Is On Fire*.)

Still, Greta and her parents listened to each other. For example, soon the whole family stopped travelling by air. (This took a lot of effort, because Greta's mother was an opera star and had to appear in different cities around the world.) And the more Greta discovered a purpose in her life, the less depressed she became. And as one member of the family began to shine, so did the others.

Some things are more important than being popular

Every day as Greta sat in front of the Parliament building, some of the members of Parliament greeted her warmly. Others, however, turned away and mocked her on social media. These negative comments multiplied quickly.

Although Greta found the situation stressful, she kept going. She realized, and said over and over, that if people didn't understand the climate crisis, then what she was doing would seem crazy to them. But that wasn't a reason to stop.

Science is important

Sometimes people say that Greta is just a child "and we shouldn't be listening to children." But Greta has been researching the science of climate change since she was nine years old. She began her school strike by handing out information about this problem. So when people say we shouldn't be listening to children, Greta says fine, "Just listen to the rock solid science instead." Which means it's a good idea to pay attention in science class. It's probably going to be useful.

**GRETA'S STORY
by Valentina Camerini
(Aladdin, 2021)**

The story of the way Greta challenged politicians and the way her family cared for her and learned how to support her is beautifully and respectfully told in language that everyone can understand. Sometimes Greta feels like a faraway person doing things nobody else could ever do. This book makes you feel as if you know her.

FIVE

HANNAH BYWATER AND SIMON JACKSON

CARE FOR ANIMALS IN DANGER

annah's Story

It was Christmas morning. Hannah Bywater was excited about her gift from her Aunt Lori and Uncle Johnny. Hannah was six years old and she loved her new stuffed sea turtle, which had soft, floppy legs. Along with the cuddly toy, her aunt and uncle explained that they had adopted a sea turtle in her name. They also explained why they had done it.

Hannah was entranced. She didn't want sea turtles – the real, swimming ones – to be endangered, so she got to work. First, she learned everything she could about them, and then she raised money by making friendship bracelets and organizing bake sales and lemonade stands. For her seventh birthday, instead of more gifts, she asked for donations for a turtle sanctuary in Northern Bali. "I figured I already had a sufficient amount of things," she says now.

That year she raised $305. The following year she raised $2,000. By now Hannah was caring for more than turtles (although she still loved them.) Soon the money she raised was being used to build an artificial reef to help grow back damaged coral in Bali, and to plant trees for endangered orangutangs on the neighbouring island of Sumatra.

Hannah spent the rest of her childhood and teen-age years bringing news about endangered species in other parts of the world back to her home city of North Bay, Ontario. Throughout this whole time, she continued to speak to students and service clubs about turtles in Bali and orangutangs in Sumatra, and she continued to raise thousands of dollars to help these vulnerable creatures live.

Twelve years after she was given a stuffed toy and a story to go with it, Hannah is standing in front of the city council of her hometown. She is asking them to save the nearby home of some Blanding's turtles – a turtle at risk right here in Canada – from construction that is happening on the turtles' protected wetland.

Hannah speaks through tears at first. It is clear this is a matter of the heart for her, and for the crowd that fills the chamber. "We love you Hannah," someone shouts. Everyone can see that Hannah knows what she is talking about. She quotes famous people, many of whom she has met. "I never thought that I would be pleading for the protection of our own protected species, in our own protected wetland," she says. The wetland is part of an ancient portage. It is also environmentally precious, and Hannah wonders how this council thinks they have "more knowledge and expertise than the experts" who have declared it too valuable to destroy.

Hannah is indeed beloved in this city. Everyone is proud of her wonderful work around the world. The mayor lets her talk a little beyond the ten minutes each speaker is allowed, which almost never happens. The crowd stands and cheers for her.

But after all this, the council voted to allow construction to continue on the turtles' home. Hannah's speech should have melted the hearts of the councillors. It probably did for some. But the vote still didn't go the way the Hannah and those who were trying to defend the turtles wanted.

imon's Story

Simon Jackson was on a camping trip in Yellowstone National Park with his parents. They camped a lot, all around North America. He was just seven years old, but he waited patiently at a lookout until he saw a big, beautiful mother grizzly bear and her cubs. It was a wonderful moment, one he never forgot. Not even when he was back home in Canada.

Besides their love of camping, Simon's family also loved to discuss current events. Once, they heard a news story about plans to cut down the forest home of Kodiak bears in Alaska. Simon wanted to help, and he spent that summer selling lemonade on their front lawn. He raised $60 for the World Wildlife Fund and wrote to the American president and the Canadian prime minister asking them to help the bears. A few months later, Simon got a letter in the mail. The Kodiak bear was saved! In his excitement, Simon felt pretty sure he was responsible for the change.

Years later, as he got older, he understood that a letter from one child doesn't very often change the mind of a powerful politician. It took a lot of people who were also trying to save the bears' home to do that. But, just like Hannah and the sea turtles, Simon had learned to stand up and speak out for the creatures he loves.

When he was 13, Simon decided to focus on the Kermode bear, a rare white bear, sometimes called the spirit bear. It is found only in a certain part of the rainforest in British Columbia, which is where Simon lived. This forest was under great stress from logging. When he heard about the danger they were facing, Simon was first shocked, then filled with passion to save their home. He gathered friends and classmates and started writing letters. He made speeches. The group became larger and larger, with millions of people around the world trying to save the home of the white bear. It also had a name – the Spirit Bear Youth Coalition. They made ornaments to sell as fundraisers, organized students in countries far away, donated money and stamps, stuffed envelopes, made more speeches, and wrote letters.

But it was complicated. Many different groups got involved in the issue – politicians, environmentalists, corporations, First Nations – and they had many different ideas about what was best. And while the white bears actually lived in just one area, many people were trying to preserve a much bigger part of the West Coast. Delicate and long-lasting negotiations took place with all the different groups that were involved, over how best to manage logging while protecting the forest and the waterways and the people who lived and worked there. Sometimes the beautiful white bears themselves almost got lost in all the politics, which was very hard for Simon.

But Simon's group kept pushing hard to protect the bear's habitat. The struggle went on and on. When this happens, sometimes all sides can get stuck in their arguments. Finally, "to get the bear saved," says Simon now, "the Youth Coalition had to cease existing." You can imagine how hard that was to do. It worked, though. New voices, a broader movement, and "endless amendments" in the final agreement resulted in safety for the bears.

Did they get 100% of what we asked for? "No," says Simon. "But something like 92%, which is more than I ever thought possible." It had taken two decades, 20 years, but finally the rare white bears had the land and the trees and the salmon and the space they need to live.

WHAT WE CAN LEARN FROM
SIMON AND HANNAH

If people were more able to build trusting relationships, it would have been easier. If we all grew up knowing and understanding nature, it would have been easier. If there was some way we could learn to love each other and Mother Earth, that would be great. Here's how we can do this.

Avoid seeing enemies (unless they are)

If you think of your favourite classes at school, there is probably a lot of talking back and forth, kids and teachers sharing opinions and even joking until they finally get to a point where every student understands the lesson. At its best, talking to the government and other organizations can be like that. There's a lot of discussion in a strong democracy. The whole idea is that questions are asked and the strongest possible arguments are offered. We try to persuade one another about what is good. Sometimes it doesn't work, but then it is important to try to figure out *why* it didn't work.

It's also important to think of those who oppose you simply as people who are committed to another point of view. You don't agree in this matter. Maybe tomorrow, on another, you will. That does not mean you stop telling the truth and standing up to them. It certainly doesn't mean you stop fighting for what you love and believe in, like the right to vote. It's

---

GROUPS TO SAVE ANIMALS

Starting your own group at your school is something almost anyone can do. That often begins with a project. For example, at Parry Sound Public School in Ontario, the Grade 4 students and their teacher, Joshua Dawson, made little spotted owls from felt, and learned a lot about one of Canada's endangered species. They did this because they had read a terrific book, *Awesome Wildlife Defenders,* by Martha Attema (Ronsdale Press). It tells the story of Rebecca, who is 11. She has a mom who is a writer, a best friend named Frieda, and a really good teacher who often speaks in rhyme. Rebecca also has panic attacks. And she loves owls. When she and a quiet (but very smart) classmate named Cedar work together on a project, good things eventually happen for everyone, even owls. You can find out more from http:// www.marthaattema.com

The Canadian Wildlife Federation

The CWF has many animals you can adopt, just as Hannah adopted sea turtles. You can cuddle up to a moose or a

just that people who disagree with you don't have to be your bitter enemies. You can think of them as adversaries. When Hannah spoke to the city councillors about the turtles, with all her supporters around her, she was not speaking to enemies. They were adversaries in a democracy where things can change. Perhaps if the councillors had grown up knowing (like Hannah) the importance in our world of every creature, including small yellow-throated domed-shelled turtles from an ancient lineage, they might have voted differently.

---

beaver at night, a snowy owl, or a pelican, and more. When you turn 15, you can join Wild Outside, which is free for 15- to 18-year-olds who want to do shoreline cleanups or habitat restoration or other projects and meet new friends. https://tinyurl.com/yckw3mnw

Hannah's Planet
Hannah Bywater can always use your help saving sea turtles and orangutangs, and fundraising is one way to do that. To learn how (and find out more about her), go to hannahsplanet.ca

Nature Labs
is the creation of Simon Jackson, who worked hard for the spirit bear, and Jill Cooper. Together, they have worked for years to create an online high school classroom full of storytelling and powerful multimedia, to help students connect to the land and to the animals that inhabit it. And to think critically. And to heal our democracy. Watch the introductory video at https://tinyurl.com/3b3bdw5d or visit https://naturelabs.ca

Use your power and get attention

Of course, you still need to educate and change minds and stop damage. That is why youth need the vote. As Simon says, "When young people take a stand, it becomes a good-news story that opens doors, makes people listen, and shines a brighter spotlight." If organizations or companies or governments are busy creating loopholes or dodging regulations (and now we *are* talking enemies), then youth can shine a light on what they are doing and demand better behaviour. Youth can create a better space and persuade politicians to move into it. Then it becomes easier for all of them to do the right thing. Educate them well. Life is long. Keep going.

Grief is allowed

All these struggles – especially those to protect vulnerable species – are matters of the heart. The world around us tells us all too often that money is all that matters. Words like "uninformed," "naïve," "economics " and "job loss" are used as weapons, especially against young activists. It is important to allow yourself to feel sad at another blow to a species in trouble. Most of all, it is important not to stop feeling, even though the thought of no more smiling turtles – which is what Blanding's turtles are often called, because that's how they look – even if the thought of no more caribou and no more narwhals hurts a great deal. We need to keep feeling our emotions. Courage is a word that comes from the Latin word *cor*, meaning "heart." If our heart gets hardened so it can't feel, then courage disappears as well. And we activists need courage to keep working and fighting for what is right.

All life is holy

Saving endangered species is about ethics, morality, and spirituality. All those big, respectable words. The planet is a giant interconnected web of life, where everything depends on everything else. You know this. If too many bees die from pesticides, many plants (including food plants such as blueberries and strawberries and pumpkins) will not be pollinated. People will go hungry. If too many songbirds disappear, people will lose sounds that make them happy. The world will be a sadder place.

The fight to preserve endangered animals is about what is fair. No species is entitled to completely destroy another species. We are all related. Humans only exist because we live on a planet that has just the right amount of water and just the right amount of sunlight and just the right amount of oxygen to turn tiny cells into giant redwoods and giraffes and sage grouse and elephants and whales and us. It took billions of years for all this to happen, but here we are. Some call it a miracle. When any of us finds the heart to help save a creature facing extinction, perhaps we have found our own spirituality.

Try to find a balance

When we are in a many-sided argument, it is important to find balance. This may be the hardest thing of all. Balance means working and working, trying very hard to be fair, until you find a way to meet everyone's needs. Not necessarily everyone's *wants*, but their *needs*. People and nature, both. After all the struggles to save the Kermode bears, the premier of British Columbia declared the agreement they reached a "byproduct of compromise." But Simon says he's "never been a fan of compromise; I'm more a believer in balance, and though the difference between balance and compromise is small, it's important." Balance, he says, allows for "innovation and patience to win the day, and usually ensures bottom lines are upheld."

The bottom line for Simon was saving the home the white bears needed. The process to get there was complicated and flawed. According to Simon, we need to learn from those flaws. Most of us do not have "nature literacy," a keen ear to hear and understand what nature is trying to tell us. In spite of that, the spirit bears' home, and a buffer of forest around it, is safe. People did try to talk to one another, and often succeeded. Fresh thinking is difficult when negotiations take years. Patience is strained when your heart is at stake. But the resulting balance – even if it looks wobbly sometimes – is good.

A VOICE FOR THE SPIRIT BEARS
by Carmen Oliver, illustrated by Katy Dockrill

When Simon Jackson was seven, he waited and waited at a lookout point until he saw a grizzly bear and her two cubs. That was the beginning. He read about bears and then, when he was 13, he discovered that the Spirit Bears, found in the Great Bear Forest, were in trouble. He began to write letters. Even though he stuttered and it was hard to do, he made speeches. This is an inspiring book, filled with lovely, playful paintings. You can see Simon reading https://tinyurl.com/mvaknx4z

Who knows how many creatures around the world we can save. Nobody knows what the future will bring. But one of the many things activists do well is watch. They stay alert. And they call out those who stray over the line, because the bears (or the turtles or the water or the climate) are what counts.

SAVING
THE
FUTURE

Activists do know this: Working on painful problems, gathering others to help, and learning how to use your voice to protect what you love – turtles, orangutangs, bears, water – give us meaning and strength. And that strange emotion called hope.

SIX

ROBIN WALL KIMMERER

CHOOSE THE RIGHT WORDS

When Robin Wall Kimmerer was a little girl, she would go canoe camping with her family in the Adirondack mountains in New York state. She loved the birdsong and the mists rising off the lake at sunrise, and then the words of gratitude spoken by her father to the mountain. Every day began the same way, with Robin and her brother and sisters becoming quiet just before breakfast. They would watch their father go to the edge of their campsite to make an offering. He would pour some of the steaming, wonderful-smelling coffee from the smoke-blackened pot onto the ground. "Here's to the gods of Tahawus," he would say.

Today, Robin is a a writer and biology professor. She tells that camping story in her book *Braiding Sweetgrass*. At the time, she thought that no other family began their day the ways hers did. But she knew it was about being grateful. Her family, she explains in the book, was saying to the land and to the mountain named Tahawus, "Here we are," and the land was murmuring to itself, "Ohh, here are the ones who know how to say thank you."

Robin's story tells us that words are important.

Names are important. When we are activists, we need to know that the words and names we are using are true. Otherwise, our resistance – to climate change, to the loss of animals – means nothing. If our own words are not true, then perhaps climate change or plastic pollution are not true either. But, of course, these things *are* true, proven by evidence-based facts, detailed by people we know are wise. So we trust them and we trust their words.

Tahawus is the true name of the mountain that overlooked the campsite Robin visited as a child. Later it was called Mount Marcy, after a governor who, Robin says, "never set foot on those wild slopes." But her Potawatomi people knew its true name, Tahawus, the cloud-splitter. Her father had climbed the mountain many times. He knew it and could speak to it in a familiar way, just as we call our own grandmother "Nana," in a familiar way, even while we might call other people's grandmothers "Mrs. Smith," for example.

When Robin's people call a mountain "cloud-splitter" because it is so high, they are calling it what it really is. They honour it by seeing it properly, as people who care about it.

FIGHTING FOR WHAT WE RESPECT AND LOVE

Not far from my own home in Northern Ontario is a famous mountain. White people who mapped this area over 100 years ago named it Maple Mountain. But the Teme-Augama Anishnabai, who called this land home long before white people arrived, know its real name to be Chee-bay-jing, "the place where the spirits go."

When the Ontario government decided it would be a good idea to build a ski resort on this sacred mountain, the Anishnabai said no. They had a legal caution placed on a large area, including the mountain. That meant nobody could build on it. Many years later that caution was removed. But by then, Ontario knew it was not a good idea to turn it into a resort. Restaurants and chair lifts might be fun in certain places, but a place where the spirits go requires respect, quiet, and reverence.

Also not far from my home is small Indigenous community called Beaver House. But the community's real name is Misemaquish, "the beaver nest where the family is." When we call it by that name, we are really saying that the beaver are like us. They live as a family, with parents taking care of the children. The beaver are not just fur coats or hats.

WORDS ARE IMPORTANT

Most of us are activists because we want to save our planet. We don't want its fresh water to be filled with chemicals from fracking. We don't want its forests to be changed forever by clear-cutting. In order to prevent these things, many of us speak of our world as if it was a person. We march and dance in the streets, picket banks that lend to fossil fuel companies, and write letters to politicians because we are defending our beloved Mother Earth. We think of our planet as a "she." It is much more difficult to hurt a "she," a "mom," than an "it." Perhaps people would not be so keen to dig up vast chunks of the earth to truck away coal if they thought of it as scarring the face of our mother.

But more than names are important. So are the words used to describe everything in our world. Paige Raibmon, a history professor in British Columbia, explains how "words carry their history with them." We have to "make visible," she says, our "habits of language." She believes children should learn how to do this in school.

For instance, a teacher might describe the way Indigenous people farmed: they planted the three sisters – beans, squash, and corn – together. The teacher might say that it is quite different from *modern* ways farming. The students might then think that the Indigenous way is old-fashioned and not as good. But if the teacher says instead that Indigenous ways of farming are quite different from *European* ways of farming, then students are more likely to think of two different but equal methods of growing food.

WHEN YOU ARE CALLED THE WRONG NAME, TELL EVERYONE THE TRUTH

When people use wrong words, you can tell the true story, using true words. Like the difference between land defenders and lawbreakers. Kahsenniyo and Skyler Williams are land defenders in Six Nations of the Grand River Territory near Caledonia, Ontario. They have been trying to protect their territory from development. The mayor of Haldimand County publicly praised the police when they arrested Kahsenniyo and Skyler. The mayor said he looked forward to more members of their family being arrested and kept in jail. The Yellowhead Institute posted an open letter by the Williams family including the children. Here's what Lola, who is 14, wrote.

My name is Lola Williams – Skyler Williams is my Dad. He has been a land defender for as long as I can remember. Me and my Dad have always been very close. Our entire family has always been very close.

In some other lesson, a teacher might say that certain First Nations' lands were *lost*. (Hm. We might ask, "Where did those lands go? Into space?) Saying "were lost" is quite different from saying these lands were *taken* by white settlers. Even more clearly, a history teacher might say that white settlers *took* the land – because *taking* is a deliberate action, not something that "just happened" for no reason. In the same way you (hungry and annoyed) would not just say "my cookie was eaten" but "so-and-so ate my cookie!"

We need to use the right words to tell the whole story. If one of your classmates is from Syria, they might be able to explain the difference between "We are here because a bomb dropped on our house" (something that sounds like it "just happened" for no reason), and "We had to flee from our home and

---

I am proud of both of my parents. But right now, after reading the Haldimand Police Services Board recommendations, and then the mayor Ken Hewitt applauding the OPP [Ontario Provincial Police] for arresting my Mom, and encouraging them to go after others in my family, I'm scared. I'm scared of what this means for my grandparents, my sisters and me.

I go to school in Caledonia. The OPP have set up right across the road from my school. These are the people that shot at my Dad and arrested my Mom when she was alone. Now I have to see them every time I look out the window or go to lunch. Every time I walk out the front doors of the school, I see all these white men with guns who are being encouraged to target me and my family. I am so disappointed that the Mayor of the County that I go to school in would choose to make such hateful and dangerous comments to target teenage girls and my elderly grand-parents.

our orange trees in the garden because our own government's planes dropped bombs on us."

GIVE EVERYTHING TRUE MEANINGS

Make sure you find true meanings. Don't just settle for the words you usually hear. Sometimes, for instance, people are called *taxpayers*. Public institutions (like schools and universities) and services (like hospitals and medical treatments) are paid for by everyone's taxes, so that everyone has an equal chance to learn and grow – even those who make so little money they don't have to pay much in taxes. But we are *citizens* even more than we are *taxpayers*. Young and old, all of us. Citizens are members of a city or province or country, and they are each responsible for the *common good*. They think about what would be best *for everybody* in their city or province or country, and they try to make that happen. *Taxpayer* is a word that is absolutely too small to describe what we all really are.

Here's another example: Sometimes police, politicians, and people in charge of large corporations call Indigenous people who are defending their land and water *lawbreakers*, or even *criminals*. That usually happens when Indigenous people try to stop a corporation from building a pipeline or a mine or cutting trees on their land – land they never "ceded" or "surrendered" but that the government has said corporations can use anyway. When Indigenous people protest, the companies get a court order telling them to stop. If they don't stop protesting, then the police are usually called in to move or arrest the protesters, which they now call criminals and lawbreakers. But really, they are *land defenders*, or *water protectors*, because they trying to keep their land and animals and water safe from harm. They are not lawbreakers. In fact, sometimes those big companies ignore environmental regulations. That makes *them* the lawbreakers.

Another example. Sometimes politicians describe people (it could be your parents or teachers) as *stakeholders* in education. Or they might describe students as *consumers* of education. Try to educate these leaders. You are a *student*. You are not simply "consuming" knowledge someone has decided you should know. You are studying – discussing, thinking, growing, learning, absorbing, analyzing, and developing. All these things happen in the classroom, but they can also happen when you're acting in a drama onstage in the school auditorium, or playing on the basketball court, or performing with the school land. As Nahira Gerster-Sim, one of the founders of Vote16BC, says, youth need to have a say in what affects them, rather than simply consuming what someone else says, or says they need. Indigenous rights, for example. "Even when we have a topic about Indigenous people, we don't hear it from an Indigenous perspective."

Young people need to be true students who help decide what will be important for the future. So try to use the right words. Even if those are words that are not used very much, search for the biggest meanings you can.

Perhaps it is actually easier to learn the true words when we are very young. We love the moon that shines outside our window at night; or we love the maple tree whose leaves sing us to sleep on a windy evening. So we love our Sister Moon and Mother Earth. Sometimes we forget this as we grow up, and just talk about the moon and the planet. But there's hope. When people happily feed the birds in winter, perhaps they are remembering the days when they knew them as our feathered brothers and sisters, our relations.

WE ARE WATER PROTECTORS by Carole Lindstrom, illustrated by Michaela Goade (Roaring Brook Press, 2020)

You will love the powerful pictures in this book. It tells the story of one young girl standing against the black snake, who, it was foretold by her people many years ago, would come and hurt the water. Now she says, "The black snake is here." But she and the other water protectors will "fight for those who cannot fight for themselves, the winged ones, the crawling ones, the four-legged, the two-legged … " These are examples of the true names for pipelines, and for animals.

SEVEN

SHANNEN KOOSTACHIN

BE A
LEADER

Shannen Koostachin and her friends from Attawapiskat, an Indigenous community in Northern Ontario, had come to Ottawa to plead for a new elementary school. They had already been promised one by the government. Their old school, where they started kindergarten, was seriously contaminated and unhealthy because of a fuel oil spill right under it. For years, the children got sick from the fumes. Eventually, they were moved to temporary classrooms in trailers.

But by now Shannen was in Grade 8. The trailers had become permanent, run-down and mouldy. In his book *Children of the Broken Treaty,* Charlie Angus (Shannen's friend and her member of Parliament) tells the story of how Shannen's class has decided not to go to Canada's Wonderland or the Royal Ontario Museum in Toronto. Instead, for their long-awaited school trip, they chose to go to Ottawa to meet with Chuck Strahl, the Minister of Indian Affairs. Perhaps he had seen the letters the children of Attawapiskat had sent to the prime minister earlier asking for a new school. He had asked some of the children and some elders to come and talk about it.

But soon after they entered his office, the minister explained that there will be no new school. Shannen jumped up and left the room. She was very angry and didn't want to cry in front of him.

Grand Chief Stan Louttit came out to comfort her and told her that the meeting doesn't end this way, and that she needed to go back in and "be a leader."

Shannen went back in just as the minister was saying he had to go to another meeting. Along with everyone else, she shook his hand and kept her head high. "We're not going to quit," she said. "We're not going to give up."

The day Shannen met with Chuck Strahl was a National Day of Action for Indigenous People. There was a big protest march in Ottawa and the children from Attawapiskat were given a place right at the front of the march. When they reached Parliament Hill, Shannen was asked to let the crowd know exactly what had happened in the minister's office. She was frightened, but Charlie Angus said, "Just speak from the heart. You'll be okay."

So that's what Shannen did. And she was *very* okay. "Today I am sad because Mr. Chuck Strahl said he didn't have the money to build our school," she began. "But I didn't believe him." She explained how she had looked him in the eye and told him the children were not going to quit, and she "could tell he was nervous." There was a huge shout from the crowd at these words. Suddenly, a 13-year-old from a vast and beautiful part of their country that most Canadians have never seen had a kind of power that a Minister of Indian Affairs can never have. She was able to name truthfully what was not fair.

Because the situation was certainly not fair. Shannen and her friends had spent years breathing in dangerous chemicals, day after day. After years of trying to learn with headaches, dizziness, rashes, and nosebleeds, the move to portable classrooms meant years without a gym. They had to rush from one class to another in the cold. Many children wore their winter coats in class because gaps under the doors let in the cold. The winter winds that blow across the beautiful muskeg lands of Attawapiskat are frigid.

Every child has a right to an education. Shannen knew that. Even though she was now in Grade 8 and wouldn't be in those freezing trailers any longer, she wanted the younger children to have something better. She didn't want any children in Grade 5, for example, dropping out. As Cindy Blackstock, an adult fighting for the rights of Indigenous children said, "When she looked at her friends, she saw hope and potential, and she saw the injustice of what they were facing."

Six years after that meeting in Ottawa, the children of Attawapiskat finally got their new elementary school, in 2014. Shannen and her friends had

---

WHAT CAN WE DO?

Shannen's friend Cindy Blackstock runs the First Nations Child and Family Caring Society. The society can tell you all kinds of things you can do alone or as a class to carry on Shannen's dream of good schools for every Indigenous child. And there's a great online book that you can find there called *Shannen's Dream: Safe and Comfy Schools.*

https://tinyurl.com/5n6h9bpa

inspired hundreds of non-Indigenous children from all over Canada and the world to write to the government, asking for it. She had made speeches from the heart. She and her friends had written to the United Nations. Shannen had been nominated for the International Children's Peace Prize.

But Shannen never saw the new school. She died in a car accident on a northern highway in the winter in 2010. She was 15, living hundreds of kilometres away from her family so that she could get a good education. She wanted to be a lawyer to fight for the education rights of First Nations children.

Even after she died, though, the children of Attawapiskat and their friends kept speaking from the heart. They started Shannen's Dream, a campaign to get good schools for all First Nations. In 2012, the government unanimously adopted Shannen's Dream in the House of Commons, promising to make First

---

WRITING A LETTER CAN HELP

A big part of Shannen's power came from the letters she and her friends wrote. And when other non-Indigenous children heard about their mouldy school, they wrote to support Shannen and her friends. They wrote to the government. They also wrote to the children in Attawapiskat. When letters arrived from children all over Canada, with hand-written messages and pictures they had drawn for them, the Attawapiskat children began to feel loved by them. And when you feel loved, you feel even braver and more determined than you already are. You can do big things. After Shannen and her sister Serena and others spoke up bravely at meetings, more adults got on board too. These adults brought money and organizers with them. Not long after, the government finally gave in. Shannen and Serena and their friends had won their school.

Nations education, at a minimum, equal to that of provincial school systems.

That was over ten years ago. As her friend Charlie Angus said in the House of Commons, on the tenth anniversary of that motion, Shannen's Dream is still the largest youth-driven children's rights campaign ever in Canada. Children and adults are still working to make sure every child has what Shannen wanted: a safe and comfy school.

Shannen is still teaching us what every young activist needs to know.

WHAT WE CAN LEARN FROM SHANNEN

First, *Shannen always spoke the truth*, clearly, from her heart. People listen when children do that. Perhaps they are tired of words that are rehearsed and slide over what's true. Children have not had time to learn how to do that. They just say what they know.

Second, *Shannen stood up even when she was nervous* and trusted that the words would come. Thousands of people were at that protest march in Ottawa. But she found her courage and spoke the words that gave them strength and courage too.

Third, *Shannen refused to accept excuses* from a leader who wouldn't do what was just and right. The Minister of Indian Affairs knew that he was responsible for education in Indigenous communities. Agreements, called treaties, were signed long ago which made his obligations very clear. He also knew – or should have known – that according to the United Nations, education is a human right, a *child's* right. Three ministers had promised a new school, but it never arrived. When this one told the little group of children and elders in his office that he didn't have enough money for a new school, Shannen said, "That's not good enough."

Fourth, *Shannen stood up for others*. She fought for a school, not for herself – because she was graduating – but for her people. She did not want younger children dropping out of school. Then she went on, with her friends, to lead other children and adults, Indigenous and non-Indigenous, from all over Canada so that the children of Attawapiskat could have a good education.

Fifth, *where you live is as special as anywhere else.* Very often people describe places like Attawapiskat as "remote." They want us to know that it is far away from big cities, which is true. But "remote" does not mean "less important." Anyone who lives in Attawapiskat or Neskantaga or Kawawachikamach is just as important as anyone who lives in Toronto or Montreal. They are entitled to as good an education as children who live in big cities.

IF NOT TO SCHOOLS, WHERE DOES GOVERNMENT MONEY GO?

It seems logical that Indigenous education – for which they are responsible – would be one of the most important things the federal government could spend money on. Instead, sometimes the money from the taxes Canadians pay is spent on projects that we now know are harmful and that should be shut down. For example, subsidies (money to support large, already-rich companies) from the federal government to the fossil fuel industry in Canada amounted to at least $18 billion in 2020. Here's where some of that money was spent:

$5.25 billion went for the very disputed Trans Mountain Pipeline in British Columbia and Alberta.

$500 million went for loans to the very disputed Coastal GasLink (CGL) pipeline in British Columbia

$13 million went for policing costs, to prevent Indigenous land defenders from protecting their own land from the CGL pipeline.

EIGHT

VIJAY TUPPER

WORK TOGETHER

Vijay Tupper was at a town hall meeting in his city of Burnaby to discuss both climate change and a pipeline. He was 11 years old, and he had never before spoken in front of 200 people. But he was scared about the damage an oil spill would do, so he got to his feet. "I was," he says now, "stressed out of my mind. I didn't know if I could string two words together." But he spoke passionately about what could happen. When he stumbled over a word, someone in the crowd yelled it out for him. He even got a quote in the media afterwards: "In case of a spill, the ground would be covered in brown goop."

"There was not much an 11-year-old can do except raise their voice," he says five years later. So he did that, trying to hold his member of Parliament – who was hosting this meeting – to account. Since then, Vijay has worked very hard and has learned a great deal about meeting together and organizing and creating actions that make people consider climate change seriously. He is convinced that activist young people need to work together, that "five people get a lot more done than just one." In fact, "networking is a huge part of organizing," he says. "There comes a point where you need to start connecting with people who are like-minded, who do the things you do."

When Vijay was 14, in 2019, he started making those connections. A school project put him in touch with a member of the Vancouver-area group called Sustainabiliteens. This group of teens was worried that if the forces behind the breakdown of the world's climate aren't stopped, "this chaos" in the words of their website, "will become our new reality."

Vijay joined them. Sustainabiliteens has done some thinking about the state of the climate and has developed clear statements. They know that it is possible to stop climate disasters, by using wind and solar power and great public transportation and bike lanes and – really important – by paying more attention to the voices of people still in school who will have to live in the chaos ahead. They know that humans have to change the way they live and work – the economy – because it "harms workers and all life on earth," and allows just a few people to become very rich while "the rest of us face an uncertain future."

It seems like a big job. But in their few years as a group, Sustainabiliteens has done a lot. In January 2019, they gathered at Vancouver City Hall to cheer for the councillors who voted, unanimously, to declare a climate emergency. In March of the same year, they organized 2,000 students to take to the streets for the climate march (along with 1.4 million other students around the world). In May, they got 3,000 people in Vancouver to come out for another march.

Then, on September 27, some Sustainabiliteens organized another climate march. Vijay took part, although he was not an organizer for this one. It was quite a day. They meant to start with speeches at city hall. But they had not imagined the huge number of eager marchers who began to arrive. They just watched in shock as they set up their information booth in the midst of crowds gathering at 10:30 am for an event that wasn't meant to start until 1:00 pm. More and more and more people kept arriving. By the time the speeches they had planned began, nobody could hear. Finally, they simply started to march, over 100,000 people pouring on and on

---

WHAT DO YOU BELIEVE?

Sustainabiliteens worked together to figure out what they believe in, and they try to always live that out. They remain non-violent even while they take action. They understand that we live on stolen land, within an old and very unfair system that needs to be dismantled. They agree that they will not give up, despite the fear and grief that we all feel in our day-to-day lives.

What do you believe? Here's a yes or no list of things to think about if you are planning ways to make the future safer.

Are marches and demonstrations actually important?

Can we help people who are working in fossil fuels if they want to switch jobs?

Is your own story of trying to make change important enough to share?

Is kindness as important as the anger that keeps you going?

Should your group only accept people who are experienced and very capable?

Is it possible to be joyful in the middle of all this work?

Now go to https://www.sustainabiliteens.org/ to see what Sustainabiliteens think about these things.

over one of Vancouver's bridges like a peaceful climate army.

When they finally arrived at their destination, the intersection of Vancouver's Hamilton and Georgia streets, speeches were made. Friendships formed. Reporters reported. And everyone listened to their simple message: children and teens want climate justice. After the previous summer, with smoke from wildfires drifting through the city, they wanted politicians to take climate change seriously.

A few months later, the Sustainabiliteens, along with everyone else, would be locked down in the middle of a pandemic. So they moved to Zoom and group chats, keeping their meetings on track but, as Vijay says, not being "terribly formal." It worked.

Eventually, the lockdowns began to lift. By fall of 2021, right after the federal election, Sustainabiliteens along with Fridays for Future and Extinction Rebellion (yes! all working together) brought 500 people to Canada Place on Vancouver's waterfront. They

---

THIS BOOK IS ANTI-RACIST by Tiffany Jewell, illustrated by Aurélia Durand (Frances Lincoln, 2020)

This excellent book of "20 lessons on how to wake up, take action and do the work" is terrific reading for anyone who wants to work, all colours, together. It explains words like colonialism and racism fully, over the course of the whole book. And it has a wonderful section on allyship, from the point of view of both people of privilege and people who are very often silenced. "If you are BIPoC [Black/Indigenous Person of Colour]," says Tiffany, "take up space. Sit where you like. Speak first." And if you are white, she and Vijay agree, "You can also pause before you talk. The world is used to hearing the voices and stories of white people. Change the narrative."

demanded a stop to fossil fuel expansion, a just transition away from fossil fuels, and better relations
with Indigenous people. They had speakers. And then,
with distant mountains in the background, they
handed out coloured chalk and covered a plaza with
street art, which included filling in a large design
that they had outlined earlier. "Art actions are really
good," says Vijay. They were "really terrified," he admits, "about just letting the chalk run free, but people were very respectful."

WHAT WE CAN LEARN FROM SUSTAINABILITEENS

There are a number of things we can learn from
Sustainabiliteens.

Trust, Honesty, Equality

The fact that the teens involved in Susatinabiliteens
work well together "has to do with the fact that we
are pretty honest and trusting of each other. Even
across Zoom and across four municipalities," says
Vijay. For one thing, they don't all try to do everything. "There is this level of understanding that we
entrust certain people with certain things and others with other things. It's a mostly cohesive machine
where people fit into place."

The main thing, he explains, is trust. And equality. Sustainabiliteens does their best "to avoid po-
tentially toxic systems of hierarchy, where the older
people have total control and the younger people
are alienated because they don't feel autonomy in
their work, or a choice."

Because of this trust in each other, and because

they make sure everyone has an equal voice, Sustainabiliteens is a superforce. Because they are determined to include Indigenous and Black rights, they easily use big words to express big ideas, like colonialism and reconciliation. These are, after all, connected to climate change. They believe in the power of collective action to change the world.

Honour the arts

Sustainabiliteens has done fundraisers, Vijay explains, "where we've had poets and artists. We look at the arts as pretty effective communications tools. Not everyone wants to read a long article, but people are more than happy to look at an art piece. We also use artists to attract people. Also, we can make connections to people in the community and help them financially because we typically offer honorariums. We give artists a platform. It's very deliberate and we put a lot of effort into it, and we enjoy it."

Honour the power of youth

"I think young people have an ability that many adults have lost, which is to be incredibly hopeful about the future," Vijay says. "And that comes together in this blend of motivation and optimism that

---

EFFECTIVE ACTION: TRAFFIC STOP

With a few people, you can make good use of a downtown street crossing to demand climate action. Or any other. Press the button to hold up cars. Run into the intersection and stand on the crosswalk, holding a big banner. Run back out of the intersection just before the light changes. It's possible with five or ten people, better with 15 to 25. It's not so much disturbance that drivers are angry, but it does get attention.

can drive movements and initiatives in a very sustainable way."

He believes some adults, "do activism out of sense of pessimism and helplessness or feelings of guilt. People listen to youth. We are living in this strange time where youth have so much power behind their voices. Undeniably part of that is social media." Vijay points out how Greta Thunberg changed the conversation. "Being 16 and speaking in front of the United Nations was shocking. But youth have the power, can get the platforms to do that, easier than adults might have."

Also, children and youth are more flexible in their thinking, not "trapped in their ways in understanding the world – at how they look at economics, and how climate action will impact their system of economics. People my age are a little better at breaking free from those constraints of prejudice and predisposition to certain ideas."

Be a good ally

According to Vijay, "this is the number one question in the climate movement right now. A lot of it starts with remembering that you (assuming you are a white person) hold a lot of privilege automatically. You receive benefits that other people don't. Not to say all white people in Canada and the U.S. are treated fairly or equally, but disproportionately Indigenous and people of colour bear the brunt of the crises we are facing." He suggests that "all your work should be done trying to keep that in mind."

Most of all, think before speaking. "Remember why you are doing what you are doing, and who you are doing it for. Make sure you centre them and give them time to speak and share their thoughts and knowledge. Far too often we say, 'Oh we did this with Indigenous people,' but then we never give them the opportunity to speak for themselves."

Know when to rest

The good thing about being part of an organization and working together is you don't carry everything on your shoulders. No matter how important it is. Because the cost of being a young activist can be high. This year Vijay is taking a break from the 250 to 300 hours he has spent in the last year and a half "doing more than just school, a sport, and an extra-curricular." He's not complaining. But it's hard to balance. And then there's knowing that "things are really bad right now all over the world, for every-one, in every conceivable way. It's not pleasant be-ing 16 and having that kind of knowledge.

"Learning to say no is a big part of organizing," he says. He admits he's still not good at resting. But "if you burn yourself out, you are not helping any-body."

**EFFECTIVE ACTION:
ELECTION ENDORSEMENTS**

Don't start with this, advises Vijay, because it is difficult, a lot of work, and it takes connections. During an election campaign, talk to the most worthy candidates. Carefully research their positions on the things that matter. With all the strength of your organization, publicly endorse those who stand up to a very serious screening. Follow up by sending volunteers, attending events, door knocking, canvassing to help their campaign.

NINE

DONNA SINCLAIR

DISCOVER AND DEFEND WHAT IS SACRED

It is summer in Northern Ontario, and there are puppies to play with on the dock. Four-year-old Donna was very happy. One of her aunts had been teaching her to swim, and the water welcomed her. Already she could paddle like the puppies do and keep her head up. She was not afraid of the water. It felt cool on this hot day, and the aunts and uncles who were visiting this small island where Donna lives were laughing together.

There were no children her age on this small island in Lake Temagami. Most days the aunts and uncles were not there, just her mom and dad. Even her older brother, who sometimes read to her, was not always there, because he was old enough to go to school. But Donna was never lonely. She had a large brown dog named Tarzan who allowed her to teach him to dance with her, although he was not very good. She had the trees to talk to – great pines much, much older than her. They listened quietly, and she could feel their wisdom. And there was always the lake. It was home to her, even though in early winter she had to be careful and wait until the ice was thick before she could walk on it.

One hot day she was in the rowboat with her dad, leaning over the side with her hand trailing in the water. She was suddenly, completely happy. She had no words for this, but she felt how the water and the boat, her father and the creaking oars and the clump of birch on the far shore, the blue sky and she herself were all one. They were all related to one another, like her aunts. They shared life together.

As Donna grew up, she put this feeling away. But it stayed with her, tucked into a memory that had no words. She kept that memory safe. It gave her strength to speak up for water and land in the years to come.

ACTIVISTS RESPECT WHAT IS SACRED

That child was me, many years ago. She appears in this book because moments like the one I experienced in the rowboat, on the water, are holy. Some people are able to live in that kind of happiness for a long time. We call them mystics. Others, like me, may have only moments, perhaps while looking up at a sky full of stars, or while holding a new baby – perhaps a brother or sister – in their arms. But I think that whenever we fight to save the climate, or march to save Black and Indigenous lives, or try to save a river from a pipeline, we are somehow in touch with those memories.

Earlier in this book, Sophia Mathur advises activists to "find your passion." Passion is what helps us spend time on not-always-fun Zoom calls or in meetings, writing letters, making posters, or doing whatever needs to be done. We may not always recognize our memories in our passion. All I knew, for instance, when I was part of a group that was trying to save our beautiful clean Trout Lake from a risky oil spill, was anger. It was not until later that I began to understand that this anger – this passion – came out of my own long-ago happiness, in a boat, on the waves, with my hand running through beautiful clean water. It was a different lake. But it is the same planet. The water falls as rain and rises into clouds and goes where it will. It is sacred. It is a gift from the Creator, for whom we humans have many different names.

HOW ACTIVISTS CAN HONOUR WHAT IS SACRED

Listen to sacred stories

Activists don't have to be religious. Some people belong to a church or synagogue or mosque or attend temple. Many don't. They write letters for gay rights or they take part in street theatre or tree planting days because they love justice, not necessarily

---

SACRED WATER

If you believe that water is sacred, you can try to protect it many ways.

Stop a pipeline. Spilled oil is very bad for waterways,. Even the construction of pipelines releases sediment and contamination. If a pipeline is being built near you, join a group that is resisting it.

Stop bottled water sales. That's what Mireta Strasberg-Salmon did at her high school. She and a friend campaigned to stop bottled water in vending machines. They researched the harm done by the plastic (a lot of it ends up in lakes and rivers and oceans) and the harm to communities from which groundwater is taken. It took time, but soon her high school and then all the other high schools in Burnaby, B.C., got rid of bottled water.

because a faith community says they should.

But religions tell stories. They give us words to capture those times when we are speechless with the beauty of the stars or the smooth feel of cool water when we dive into it. When I hear the story (from my own faith) of Jesus beginning his own years of activism by wading headlong into a river and emerging from it dripping and joyful and determined, it helps me feel I am not alone. I too am joyful and determined, because of water.

Another thing. After he had dunked in the water with such ceremony, Jesus set out to change the world. He made friends with fishers and Roman soldiers and poor people. He didn't try to do it alone. Just as Nahira and Vijay say earlier in this book, he

---

HELP END "BOIL WATER" ADVISORIES

After one year, a boil water advisory is called "long-term." Some last a very long time. As this book was being written, Neskantaga First Nation in Northern Ontario has had to boil their water since 1995. Which means that anybody younger than 26 does not know what it is like to drink water from the tap, or even just brush your teeth with it. The good news is 119 long-term advisories have been ended. The bad news is 43 long-term advisories remain. We can encourage politicians who are working on water treatment plants for First Nations.

Write to the Minister of Indigenous Services in Ottawa and explain how important it is for this to be done right away.

We might even challenge a politician to join us in trying to live with a boil water advisory for one week: boil (one minute, rolling boil) all the water you need for drinking, cooking, making ice cubes, brushing your teeth, washing your vegetables, and feeding your pets. If you have a baby brother or sister, the water to bathe them must be boiled first. When the week is done, talk with the politician about what the week was like.

knew it was best to work with others.

The stories found in religion are worth listening to – carefully.

Be kind and respectful

As activists, we seek to draw people together in love, not divide them. Even though we often have to shout to make ourselves heard, we do not ridicule. Furthermore, activists decide how they want to be. In the words of British Columbia's Sustainabiliteens, "We are a strong and supportive community." This means that "We take care of ourselves, each other, and our shared home. We work to cultivate strong relationships."

Listen to those who know
the land and water

Mary Laronde grew up on Kaweskakwaw Minising, an island in Lake Temagami. She is Teme-Augama Anishnabai, the deep-water people whose territory contains the island where I lived as a child. She explains that the world's most ancient water is in Temagami, and she worries about how logging and mining the land surrounding it would damage it. "Everything doesn't have to be taken," she says. "We have to get together and develop a shared land ethic."

I believe my body knows the power of that water. I listen very carefully and quietly to whatever Mary says about n'Daki Menan, the water and land of the Teme-Augama Anishnabai. That is because I am one whose connection with it is new and frail – hardly two generations old – and I need to learn how to help take care of it. When Mary says it is time to "implement our stewardship laws," and says that this water should be a world heritage site, I listen and agree. I am grateful to Mary and to this water.

Pray

Perhaps this is a new idea to you. Perhaps your family and friends do not believe that praying does anything. Lots of wonderful people have that point of view. But in my place of worship someone offers the prayers of the people every Sunday morning when we get together. One reason is because we think God loves us and listens for our words. But another reason we pray that kind of prayer is because people can't always find the right words at the right moment. So one of us sits and thinks about that, ahead of time, and then writes a prayer. As an activist, you have already been thinking about something that needs to be healed in our world. So if your family goes to church or synagogue or mosque or temple, you could write such a prayer, and offer to say it out loud, with some of your group or alone. This is how you might do it.

First, it is polite and very necessary to thank the Creator for all the good things. That's the first part of a prayer. Only after that do we ask for help with what needs to be fixed. It's like Robin, in Chapter Six, knowing that the mountain named Tahawus saw their morning offering and said to itself, "Ohh, here are the ones who know how to say thank you."

Of course, if you believe in praying, there's no reason why you can't pray silently, any time, or out loud at certain times. For instance, I generally pray for Mother Earth at mealtimes, because I am already busy saying thank you for the food and the people who grew it. So I might also say, "please help save the oceans," for instance. It's not because God needs to be told that. God knows about oceans. I do this because it helps me remember who I am - someone who cares about our planet.

Study the land

Walk in the forest if you can. Try to learn to swim, so the water can welcome you. After that, try to learn to row or paddle, if you can get to a boat or canoe or kayak. Many cities are built on the edge of a lake or a river, or they have ravines running through them, or parks and urban forests. Wherever you live - country or town or city - do your best to get to where Earth herself can speak to you. This takes persistence and a helpful, trustworthy adult. But in time you will be able to hear the language of those trees and rivers.

Dream. Wait. Reflect. Talk.

Every culture has ways to help someone figure out what they are supposed to do. Some people dream and wait to hear what the dream says. Some people sit and think, maybe with a pen and paper to write down what is good or not good about a plan. Some people talk to friends or elders they love and respect.

And then they decide how to protect what they love. Maybe it is a river, trees, beautiful old buildings, prairie grasses, farmland, people without homes, turtles whose home is in danger, a park, democracy itself.

If you are fortunate, someone in your family will teach you all this. Often that teaching happens around the dinner table, which in some traditions is a sacred place. It is where thanks are offered for the food that feeds the body, and where conversation is offered to feed the mind and spirit. (Simon Jackson, whom you met earlier in this book, says one of the gifts his parents gave him was discussion at dinner about the news.)

The chaos of a table with very young children is holy too. Everyone brings what they can, including joy, tears, and noise. If no one is giving this knowledge to you, you will have to go out and look for it. Perhaps you will have to wait a few years. But meantime, you can learn the skills of activism. March with others, make posters, stand in the streets with a banner. Oppose pipelines. Write a speech, try to deliver it, be nimble in your thinking.

TEN

A
FINAL
LIST

It's up to you to decide how or if you want to resist threats to the people and other creatures who live on our beautiful planet. You know best about your town or city. You can figure out what you might do. You are the one to make the best use of your own imagination. But sometimes it's good to have some ideas and possibilities in a list. You can pick and choose and change them to suit your own inspiration. If you are feeling sad or worried about the future, sometimes just working on ideas can fill you with energy and make you feel determined and brave.

FORM AN ORGANIZATION

Invite a friend over, or two or three, who are as determined as you are. Maybe a history class made you want to support Indigenous rights. Or maybe a flood or a wildfire near you made you want to fight climate change. Or maybe you are just so angry about a foolish government decision (Yank out all the electric car recharging stations? Tear down windmills? Fund a pipeline?) that you want to vote, now. Then talk about what you can do. Start simply, maybe with a class project. Maybe have a lunchtime meeting and publicize it, which might give you a few more people. Together, give your group a name. Presto! You are an organization.

Keep track of the news. Soon there will be the right moment (maybe now) to raise your voice. Then visit your MP and/or hold a rally in front of his/her/their office. Write a press release and invite the media. Make your position known. Soon your organization will grow. You are on your way. This is one way. Greta Thunberg began as an organization of one. But pretty soon, Fridays for Future had millions of members. If an organization is needed, it will live.

EDUCATE YOUR SCHOOL

You could start with a presentation or book report. Just in your class. Or contact the drama teacher and write a play to present at an assembly. Start a letter-writing campaign. Don't be shy. Write to the prime minister or the president or your member of Parliament or your representative, whoever you want. Also, you can ask your teachers to invite guest speakers to come to your class and discuss their book in English or civics or wherever it fits. Hold a rally. If your teacher or principal need convincing, you can explain that this is an essential lesson in democracy. Because it is.

MAKE ART

Make every kind of art. Create street theatre. Wear costumes, like a hazmat suit when an oil spill is a worry (benzene fumes, anyone?) and hand out leaflets. Dance in the park and invite your MP to join you. Make posters about your cause and your upcoming play or rally or march or festival. Write poems and have an outdoor (or indoor) reading. You can allow some adult poets to read too, if you like. Make a huge banner (old sheets will do) and hold it at an overpass, preferably when a dignitary who needs persuading is passing by. In your downtown, you might find a friendly building owner, who will let you can paint a mural, with permission. Find a friendly paint store to donate materials if you can.

RAISE MONEY

Don't underestimate the power of a bake sale. You can present customers with evidence of need or reasons for your cause at the same time. Conversation about climate change or children's rights is more persuasive over cookies. Get together with your grandmother and bake up a storm. (Okay. I just wanted to get that in there. You won't make a lot of money with a bake sale, but your grandmother, who loves you, will be thrilled.) Here is a handy cookie recipe.

OATMEAL COOKIES

Make ahead: *Baking Mix*

This can be doubled. Or tripled. So you always have some mix on hand for a quick fundraiser.

2 cups whole wheat flour	1 tsp baking soda
2 cups unbleached flour	1 cup brown sugar
2 tsp salt	2 cups granulated sugar
2 tsp baking powder	

Combine well in a bowl, stirring with a fork to break up lumps. Store in a covered container.

Then make: *Oatmeal Chocolate Chip Cookies*
Preheat oven to 350°F. Place 3 cups baking mix in a bowl. Add 1 cup rolled oats, 1 tsp cinnamon, and 1/2 tsp nutmeg. Add 3/4 cup very soft butter, 2 eggs, and 1 tsp vanilla. Beat about 2 minutes. Stir in 1 cup chocolate chips. Roll into 1-inch balls, flatten slightly and place on slightly greased cookie sheets. Bake about 12 to 15 minutes, until golden at edges.

Or you can set up a GoFundMe page, which may raise more money than a bake sale, and again, you state the facts of your cause. Or you can sponsor a race. Or just pass a hat, if, for example, you only need enough money to buy some posterboard for signs.

OCCUPY THE AIR WAVES

Find out when your local radio station or even the national CBC is hosting a talk show on your subject. (You can even encourage them to do so with letters and visits, if they don't seem aware of it.) On the day of the talk show, have several callers ready by their phones. Everybody start calling in before the show is on air. Be prepared with all your information and be polite. Tell the call screener your name and age, and why you are concerned. If you get on the air, be polite, informed, and personal. If you are calling about, for instance, ocean plastics, talk about your own efforts to reduce plastic, your own love of the ocean, and your own fear that whales may disappear in your lifetime – along with such facts as how much plastic is going into the water.

Local radio and television often carry public service announcements, often phone-in. You can do that too, stating who, when, where, and especially why, if you are hosting a public event that interested people can attend.

OCCUPY YOUR LOCAL POLITICIAN'S CONSTITUENCY OFFICE

Request an appointment to talk about your concern. Some representatives will welcome you, and that's good. But others may not want to hear from you at

---

DO NOT WAIT FOR HOPE

Many times before in history, people have been afraid that they were about to lose everything. All reason for hope seemed to disappear. And yet they kept going. They found tiny shreds of hope within themselves and shared it around. In Britain during World War II, bombers flew overhead night after night. Children were sent away from their parents, out of London, to live in the country to avoid being killed. Countries all over Europe had already collapsed. It seemed hopeless. But Britain did not collapse, and eventually the war ended, and the children were able to come home. In Europe, however, many other children, most of them Jewish, never got to go home. They are remembered with sorrow and love and determination. And democracy did return.

Earlier, in India, under the rule of the British, it was clear that the vast British Empire would continue forever, taking land and resources from those who had always lived there. But then Mahatma Gandhi and his followers marched to the sea, without violence, and shortly afterwards the British no longer ruled India. Other countries followed. The colonies that Britain and Portugal and France and Holland had ruled began, one after another, to break away. It was at first very surprising. Who had any hope this could ever happen? Even now, as those former colonies try to undo faulty laws and untrue stories from the past, it sometimes seems hopeless that everyone will be able to live in peace with each other. Not to mention with all the other creatures on our beautiful planet. But activists struggle on. They do not sit and wait for hope to come to them. They decide to save the future; and then they make their own hope out of stubborn hard work and imagination. It has happened before.

all. In that case, you might consider filling up their waiting room and staying. You are citizens. Be very polite – remember that the staff at the office are not responsible for government policy – but be clear that you are not going away until the member gives you a hearing. Make sure one of you keeps posting on Twitter, Instagram, etc. and lets others know where you are. Spread the word that you are here peacefully. Try to get a big crowd both in and outside the office. Produce some signs and make speeches outside. Get as much media coverage as you can.

SEND OUT A PRESS RELEASE

Make it easy for journalists to turn up or even just catch up with you after your event by sending out a press release. Write it like an article. Begin with a bold headline with the most important information. Follow with a subhead that gives a bit more information. Next, say when you need your release to be published (usually, "for immediate release"). Then say the date and location of the event and the who, what, where, when, and why of it all. Include quotes from at least two different people in your group saying exactly what you want said. (Busy journalists will paste these quotes into their story.) Include some colour (specific details, sounds, smells, etc.).

At the end, after "For further information," add the names of two spokespersons with information on how to contact them.

STEAL THE STAGE

Take advantage of being a kid. In a crowd of adults, all eyes will go to the one person who is different, which you are by being younger than everyone else.

Book time for two or three members of your group on the agenda of your town council. Prepare timed speeches (you'll be given a time limit) on different aspects of your subject (they won't let you repeat the same information). Be fact-based, but personal. State your age. Above all, bring all of your friends, aunts, uncles, neighbours, and parents who agree with you. If the meeting is about, say, a soccer field your city wants to turn into a shopping mall, wear your soccer uniform and have friends carry any trophies your team has won. If you are caring for a precious lake threatened by oil or pesticides, everybody carry paddles. If you are defending turtles, everyone could carry pictures of them, maybe taped to sticks so they can be waved. Be sure to stand quietly after speaking; expect questions. If you don't feel fully prepared to answer a particular question, just invite another one of your group to join you, saying politely that this is their area of expertise.

DEVELOP A WEBSITE

If you have a website, write a clear statement of your principles; tell a clear story. This keeps everyone looking outward. There's nothing that brings a group together more than teaching others. While you are talking to each other, and then the world, you begin to understand what you already know.

USE DIGITAL MEDIA, BUT WISELY

"The most dangerous thing about social media," says Vijay (Chapter 8), "is that it tends to lead people to being more polarized or stuck within their own groups, because you tailor your content to your sensibilities." But dividing people just makes it harder for those still learning about the climate crisis, say, to get on board. Vijay says that "climate should not have to be a hugely disputed political issue. I don't see a good reason for the right or the left to disagree on the urgency of the climate crisis and how we should go about it."

While we have to be aware of the "shocking spread of misinformation," social media has also "allowed so many more people to access the climate movement. It allows more of a platform to speak, and [makes] information more accessible even for people who are watching from the sidelines."

ENLIST ADULTS TO HELP

It is helpful to have tall or large people marching with you. If you are concerned some onlookers might respond disrespectfully, make sure every organizer is buddied with two other people, so you can watch out for each other. Make sure cell phones and cameras are highly visible. Don't forget that if you want to have speeches at your event, you will need loudspeakers, a visible place to stand, and spokespeople who are prepared to speak. Alert the police about the march ahead of time. You have a right to dissent, and their job is public safety. If anyone tries to import violence or intimidation into your protest, you are entitled to police protection.

USE YOUR IMAGINATION

Imagination is your very best tool to help you tailor your action to your local situation. If you have a lake threatened by a pipeline, rather than a march you could have everyone canoe or kayak on it. In one place where a lake was frozen, organizers asked everyone to dress in black and then to "ski the spill" – that is, to ski where the oil would flow if there was a spill, to show the world where the damage would be. Invite the press. Take lots of pictures.

IN THE END ...

Remember this: You may not succeed, but you will have loved. The best way to deal with the grief and anxiety we all might feel right now is to work together out of love for this beautiful planet. Love brings courage, and courage brings hope.

We all know that success is not guaranteed. No future is ever guaranteed. Sometimes it is shaped by blind luck. Sometimes by circumstances nobody could ever have seen coming, like a pandemic or the invention of the Internet. Sometimes the future – which eventually becomes the present, and then the past – simply bends differently. It bends towards justice and kindness and goodness because people have gathered – kids and adults – to try to find a better way. They have imagined *together*, and then have created a better future.

Many of us have been taught that a little child shall lead them in that effort.

WHAT IF:
A VERY SHORT GUIDE FOR ACTIVISTS

What if you are afraid or anxious

Quite often, if you are anxious, trying to do something about what you are concerned about – such as climate change or water in Indigenous communities – will help. Especially if you are doing it with friends, or with people who become friends.

What if the cost seems too high

If you have been working on changing the way things are for a while, you may get tired. Take a rest. Find something that makes you laugh. Go for nature walks if you can; it may help you remember what you are working for. Take a year or more off. Others will lead. "Taking a break doesn't mean the work stops," says Vijay (Chapter 8). "Someone else will step up. It is just what needs to happen so you can come back and work more."

What if you lose

Carry on. This is not over.

What if you win

Carry on. This is not over.

What if there is a catastrophe/wildfire/flood

Try to not to say I told you so, although that would be entirely understandable. Lug sandbags, help cook, do very practical things to help. Be kind. (I probably don't need to suggest any of this because you would do it anyway.)

What if your parents say no

Tell them how you feel. Wait to see what they say and listen to them carefully. Say, "You are saying ... " and repeat what they said. That way they know you heard them. (Also, you are showing them how to listen to you.) Do your best to educate them. Greta Thunberg educated her parents and they changed their lives for her. Suggest they read a book written by Greta's family called *Our House Is on Fire*. It might help them be less worried. (Mostly, parents object because they are afraid for you.) Meantime, gather your friends and start small, perhaps with an excellent class project. When you get a good mark on it, your mom and dad may start to come around.

What if you are not sure this is a good cause

There are so many ways to figure out if a protest or a letter-writing campaign is something you want to be involved with. You may want to discover the context of this protest. If you are standing with Indigenous people over their land rights, you may need to consult a history teacher you trust, so that you know the story of Indigenous land in your country. The RAVEN movement can tell you more. If you are standing against fossil fuels, you may want to consult some environmental organizations, such as Stand.Earth (www.stand.earth), or Environmental Defence Canada (environmentaldefence.ca), or Dogwood (dogwoodbc.ca), or 350.org. If you are concerned about environmental racism, you might want to do a project that helps you find more about it. After that, you will be able to figure out what you want to do.

WHAT'S THEIR PASSION?

Join up the famous activists with their cause.

Simon Jackson	Turtles
Greta Thunberg	Climate
Hannah Bywater	Voting rights
Nahira Gerster-Sim	Girls education
Sophia Mathur	Climate
Malala Yousafzai	Bears

You can see how these are all connected. When you stand up for bears and their safe home, you are also standing up for the climate, fish, and trees. When you stand up for young people who want the vote, you are also helping them make a public space in which politicians must act for LGBTQ2S rights, clean water, Black or Indigenous rights, or children's rights.

ONE: SEE CLEARLY, GET THE VOTE

Gerster-Sim, Nahira. "Why I Want the Right to Vote." *Dogwood* (April 25, 2019). https://tinyurl.com/3wa4pm9c

— "The Next Four Years and Beyond," *Dogwood* (October 6, 2020). https://tinyurl.com/2p97nx3k

Klein, Seth. "We Face So Many Crises. Let Youth Lead, Serve and Vote." *The Tyee* (June 22, 2020). https://tinyurl.com/4mybr5ve

Olaniyan, Olamide. "It's a Waiting Game for BC Teens Hoping to Get the Vote." *The Tyee* (November 26, 2019). https://tinyurl.com/yckuv3ys

"Become a Vote16BC Ambassador!" *Dogwood*. https://tinyurl.com/2p986jcs

"Vote 16 – High School Presentation." https://tinyurl.com/3f5x5y9u

TWO: KNOW YOUR RIGHTS AND FIGHT FOR THEM

Canadian Press. "Young People Taking Climate Change Lawsuit to Federal Court of Appeal." *CBC NEWS* (November 24, 2020). https://tinyurl.com/yw98xtbt

CBC Kids News. "'The Youth Have Risen!' Climate Strikers Storm the Streets." *CBC* (March 22, 2019). https://tinyurl.com/mubvf6wv

Drugmand, Daba. "Latest Youth Climate Lawsuit Filed Against 33 European Countries Over Human Rights." *Desmog* (September 3, 2020). https://tinyurl.com/mt9tfahm

Ecojustice. "Victory! Young Ontarians Prevail Over Ford Government's Attempt to Shut Down Climate Case." *Ecojustice* (November 13, 2020). https://tinyurl.com/5xczpupm

Parker, Laura. "Kids Suing Governments about Climate: It's a Global Trend." *National Geographic* (June 26, 2019). https://tinyurl.com/4te99uz4

Scaini, Stefan. "CitizenKid: Earth Comes First." *White Pine Pictures* documentary, 23 min. https://tinyurl.com/3ck6ue4c

Sharp, Morgan. "Young Activists Win Right to Sue Ontario's
Ford Government Over Climate Policy." *Canada's National
Observer* (November 13, 2020). https://tinyurl.com/2p8k72vs

Students Commission. "Children's Rights in Canada." (April
2018) pdf. https://tinyurl.com/2p9hdhwd

UNICEF. "The Convention of the Rights of the Child in Child-
Friendly Language," UNICEF Canada pdf. https://
tinyurl.com/4dpyh89u

Wood, Stephanie. "Trans Mountain Pipeline demanded teens
cover legal costs – then changed its mind." *Canada's
National Observer* (September 9, 2019). https://tinyurl.com/
4hc48hyt

THREE: BE AN ANTI-RACISM ALLY

CBC News. "Canadians Hold Protests, Vigils for Black Lives Lost
at the Hands of Police." *CBC News* (June 5, 2020). https://
tinyurl.com/bdcuc7zz

Holmes, Linda. "Thousands Attend Peaceful North Bay Black
Lives Matter March." *BayToday* (Jun 7, 2020). https://
tinyurl.com/2p9xxry7

Jewell, Tiffany. *This Book Is Anti-racist.* Illustrated by Aurélia
Duran. Minneapolis: Frances Lincoln Children's Books, 2020.

Little, Lori-Anne. "North Bay Hosts Peaceful Protest in Support
of Black Lives Matter." *CTV News* (June 7, 2020). https://
tinyurl.com/2ybpx7yn

Porter, Jody. "Indigenous People Say Racial Profiling Most Often
Felt in Stores: Human Rights Commission Report." *CBC
News* (May 4, 2017). https://tinyurl.com/3haem55c

Wilson, P. J. "2,000 March against Racism." *North Bay Nugget*
(June 6, 2020). https://tinyurl.com/yhz2c8nn

FOUR: SHOW UP

Ernman, Malena and Beata, and Greta and Svante Thunberg.
Our House Is on Fire: Scenes of a Family and a Planet in Crisis.
London: Allen Lane, 2020.

Camerini, Valentina. *Greta's Story: The Schoolgirl Who Went on
Strike to Save the Planet.* Illustrated by Veronica "Veci"
Carratello. New York: Aladdin, 2021.

Gessen, Masha. "The Fifteen-Year-Old Climate Activist Who Is
Demanding a New Kind of Politics." *The New Yorker*
(October 2, 2018). https://tinyurl.com/3treyz45

— "Greta Thunberg Is the Anti-Trump." *The New Yorker* (September 24, 2019). https://tinyurl.com/52h2cxtm

Kormann, Carolyn. "The Pure Spirit of Greta Thunberg Is the Perfect Antidote to Donald Trump." *The New Yorker* (December 13, 2019). https://tinyurl.com/mvehcuv6

Thunberg, Greta. *No One Is Too Small to Make a Difference.* London: Penguin, 2019.

— "Recently I've Seen Many Rumours … " Facebook post, Feb 11, 2019.

Witt, Emily. "Greta Thunberg's Slow Boat to New York." *The New Yorker* (August 30, 2019). https://tinyurl.com/4t8teeuh

— "How Greta Thunberg Transformed Existential Dread into a Movement." *The New Yorker* (April 6, 2020). https://tinyurl.com/yhhnhyv6

FIVE: CARE FOR ANIMALS IN DANGER

Attema, Martha. *Awesome Wildlife Defenders.* Vancouver: Ronsdale Press, 2021.

Bywater, Hannah. "Become an Activist!" *Hannah's Planet.* http://www.hannahsplanet.ca/how-you-can-help.aspx

— *Speech to North Bay City Council to Protect the Natural World,* https://tinyurl.com/mubepy3e

Groc, Isabelle. "10 Spirit Bear Facts You Need to Know." *Discover Wildlife.* https://tinyurl.com/y8fur5tr

Ignatieff, Michael. "Enemies vs. Adversaries." *The New York Times* (Oct 16, 2013). https://tinyurl.com/3wh2zwrt

Jackson, Simon. "Spirit Bear Saved." *Ghost Bear Institute.* (2016). https://ghostbear.org/spirit-bear-saved/

MacLeod, Andrew. "Finding Unity in the Great Bear Rainforest." *Hakai Magazine* (October 20, 2020). https://tinyurl.com/2p93p2sc

Oliver, Carmen. *A Voice for the Spirit Bears.* Illustrated by Katy Dockrill. Toronto: KidsCan Press, 2019.

Ronson, Joshua. *Hannah's Planet.* North Bay: Canadore College, 2016. https://joshronson.com/hannahsplanet.

www.naturelabs.ca and ghostbear.org

SIX: CHOOSE THE RIGHT WORDS

Kimmerer, Robin Wall. *Braiding Sweetgrass.* Minneapolis: Milkweed Editions, 2013.

— "Speaking of Nature." *Orion* (June 12, 2017). https://tinyurl.com/mr3kvw63

MacLeod, Andrew. "Punishment for Pipeline Protesters, but not for Pipeline Firm's Violations?" *TheTyee* (November 24, 2021). https://tinyurl.com/pef58kth

Raibmon, Paige. "How to Talk about Relations between Indigenous Peoples and Europeans." *The Tyee* (September 28, 2018). https://tinyurl.com/96s2kf9x

Williams Family. "Open Letter from the Williams Family Regarding Their Rights and Safety." *Yellowhead Institute* (October 28, 2020). https://tinyurl.com/2p8d72cz

SEVEN: BE A LEADER

Angus, Charlie. *Charlie Angus on the 10th Anniversary of the Shannen's Dream Motion.* https://tinyurl.com/5b83pmjv

— *Children of the Broken Treaty: Canada's Lost Promise and One Girl's Dream.* Regina: University of Regina Press, 2015.

First Nations Child and Family Caring Society. www.fncaringsociety.com

Obomsawin, Alanis. *Hi-ho Mistahey!* National Film Board documentary, 1:40. https://tinyurl.com/4e4vukrr
tells the story of Shannen's Dream.

Wilt, James. "The Battle for the 'Breathing Lands': Ontario's Ring of Fire and the Fate of Its Carbon-rich Peatlands." *The Narwhal* (July 11, 2020). https://tinyurl.com/2p82zum7

EIGHT: WORK TOGETHER

Laune, Aly. "Sustainabiliteens, Other Youth to Protest for Climate Action Sept. 21," *CityNews Everywhere* (September 19, 2021). https://tinyurl.com/2ak9pr6v

Moreau, Jennifer. "Burnaby Residents Pack Meeting on Pipeline, Climate Change." *Burnaby Now* (July 16, 2016). https://tinyurl.com/4z4s2zs9

Tupper, Vijay. "Attention, Jagmeet Singh – Young Voters Want a Leader Who Will Stand Up to Big Oil." *Canada's National Observer* (September 19, 2021). https://tinyurl.com/3ry84bcn

www.sustainabiliteens.org

NINE: DISCOVER AND DEFEND WHAT IS SACRED

Solidarity Team UCC North Bay. *Wet'suwet'en Witness: Environmental Justice, Racism and Northern Ontario.* https://tinyurl.com/yc5xtmdx

I n some way, this book for children and youth grew out of my earlier book for adults, *Activist Alphabet*. The support I acknowledged in that book still applies. The activists whom I have been proud to call friends for many years continue to teach me. Their wisdom and determination still shapes the world view behind *Saving the Future*.

The young people I interviewed for this book give me assurance for the future. Their courage strengthens me. Their capacity to see what needs to be done, to strategize, and to encourage and inspire in the most articulate possible way is humbling. I have tried to do justice to their work. I am incredibly grateful to Nahira Gerster-Sim, Sophia Mathur, Kile George, Kaiden Peldjack, and Vijay Tupper for the generous way they shared their time; and for their openness and trust. It took me decades to learn even part of what they already understand profoundly.

Some of the people in this book simply grew up saving the future. Simon Jackson, thanks for your patient correspondence and for the crucial, timely vision of Nature Labs. Hannah Bywater, thank you for your passionate example of what a young girl in Northern Ontario can do for ocean creatures far away.

Others in this book I have met only through their writing, their speeches, or the words of others. Shannen Koostachin, Greta Thunberg, and Robin Wall Kimmerer, became more real to me every day as I pulled books off library shelves, and searched out articles, documentaries, and YouTube conversations. I am glad to live in a world where their brilliance can be shared.

I am grateful to Martha Attema, children's author and dear friend, for ongoing encouragement and care – and especially for her early, helpful reading of a draft of this book.

So many friends listened faithfully and offered sustaining words. Peggy Walsh Craig, Trisha Mills, Adelaide Saegar, Rose Tekel, Muriel Duncan, Marg Paul, Sarah Tector, Ellen Ramsey, Jane Howe, Elizabeth Frazer, Kay Heuer, and Teresa Jones all somehow managed this in the midst of a pandemic.

Helen Rose Wabano, *miigwetch* (thank you) for your openhearted teachings, and for making Attawapiskat real to me. Mary Laronde, *miigwetch*. I rejoice in our friendship and rely on your wisdom.

Dear friends who meet at the Mother House of the Sisters of St. Joseph, and dear friends at St. Andrew's, being among you is a treasured blessing.

Wanda and John Wallace, and Kathy and Alan Aylett offered joyous birthday parties, sumptuous dinners, and all the fun of seeing their wonderful grandchildren (and ours) grow from babies to young adults. Nothing could say more strongly that the world will go on.

Wood Lake Publishing continues its work of over 40 years producing thoughtful, valuable, intelligent books. I am so proud to be one of its authors, and as always, very grateful to Mike Schwartzentruber for his stalwart, patient, trustworthy editing.

Jim Sinclair, David Sinclair, Elijah Sinclair, Andy Sinclair, Dan Vos, Tracy Sinclair, Brad Samson, Liam Sampson, Jamesie Sampson: In conversations with you over many hikes and many dinner tables, I am supported, inspired, and held to account on the matters in this book. What a magnificent family you are, and how I love you.

ACTIVIST ALPHABET
Donna Sinclair

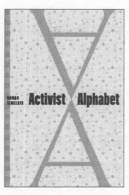

Donna Sinclair's *book Activist Alphabet* is an effort to figure out why and how activists fall passionately in love with a cause, a watershed, or a planet and its people. It's a primer, or an alphabet, on how to stay strong enough to keep putting that love into action, over and over. As Sinclair explains, it is particularly aimed at people of faith, because love, we say, is what we are about, even though it makes us terribly vulnerable to grief and loss. Good and evil, we say, is what we are about, even though that calls us to study and learn and intervene, trying to protect. Trying to find hope. Trying to see where God fits and lifts in the current chaos.

ISBN 978-1-77343-154-3
176 pages, 5.5" x 8.5" paperback, $19.95

THE ARCHITECTURE OF HOPE
Douglas MacLeod

Architect and educator Douglas MacLeod offers a stark and compelling glimpse forward to the year 2035, in which we can live and work together to build better communities for tomorrow.

This insightful and compelling book imagines the idea of cooperative communities where people can produce more energy than they use; purify more water than they pollute; grow more food than they consume; and recycle more waste than they produce, with technologies that already exist or that will be within our grasp in a few years.

Most important of all, the people of the community own and profit from these resources.

The Architecture of Hope depicts a way of living that is decentralized, re-localized, and regenerative. And possible.

ISBN 978-1-77343-174-1
80 pages, 4.75" x 7" paperback, $12.95

ALSO AVAILABLE FROM WOOD LAKE

OUR SPIRITS ALIGNED
Aboriginal Voices of Healing and Reconciliation
JoAnn Restoule, Wedlidi Speck, Karen Close

How does one define reconciliation in a way that gives meaning to those who have experienced and suffered from colonization and to those who have not? Is it even possible? This book presents a collection of storytellers who have set out to do just that. As Wedlidi Speck states in his introduction to this important book: "By sharing the stories in this book, we hope each reader will find a role in reconciliation by placing all these stories together in a mixing bowl of sorts and coming up with a broader view that will heighten our country's cultural awareness, deepen Canadian sensitivity, sharpen Canadian agility and grow cultural safety in all our country's homes, villages and work spaces."

ISBN 978-1-77343-157-4
100 pages, 4.75" x 7", paperback $12.95

WOOD LAKE

Imagining, living, and telling the faith story.

WOOD LAKE IS THE FAITH STORY COMPANY.

It has told

- the story of the seasons of the earth, the people of God, and the place and purpose of faith in the world;
- the story of the faith journey, from birth to death;
- the story of Jesus and the communities and churches that carry and treasure his message.

Wood Lake has been telling stories for 40 years. During that time, it has given form and substance to the words, songs, pictures, and ideas of hundreds of storytellers.

Those stories have taken a multitude of forms – curricula, parables, poems, drawings, prayers, epiphanies, songs, books, paintings, hymns, and more – all driven by a common mission of serving those on the faith journey.

We welcome you to join us.

WOOD LAKE PUBLISHING INC.
485 Beaver Lake Road, Kelowna, BC, Canada V4V 1S5
250.766.2778

www.woodlake.com